Where there is matter, there is geometry.

Johannes Kepler

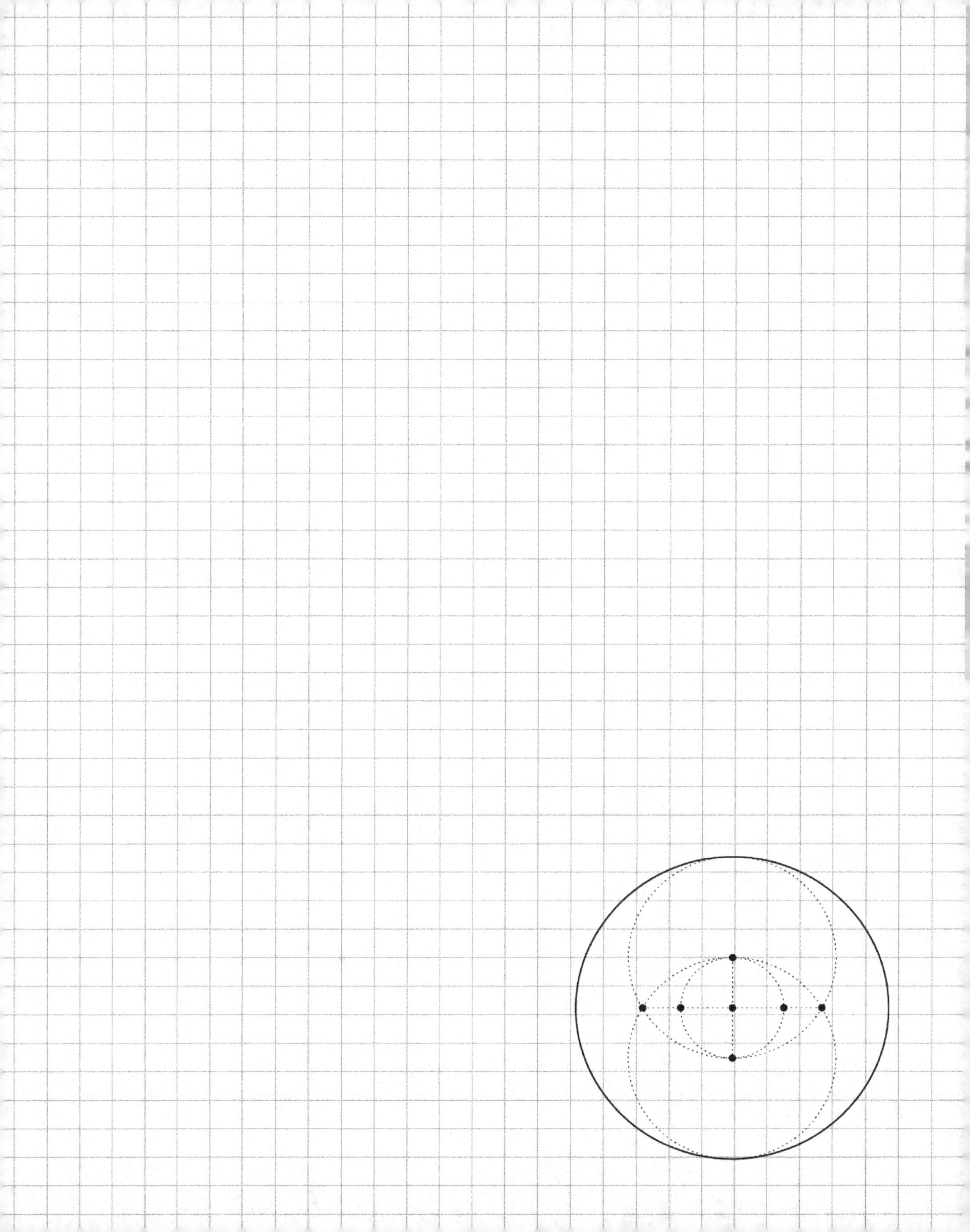

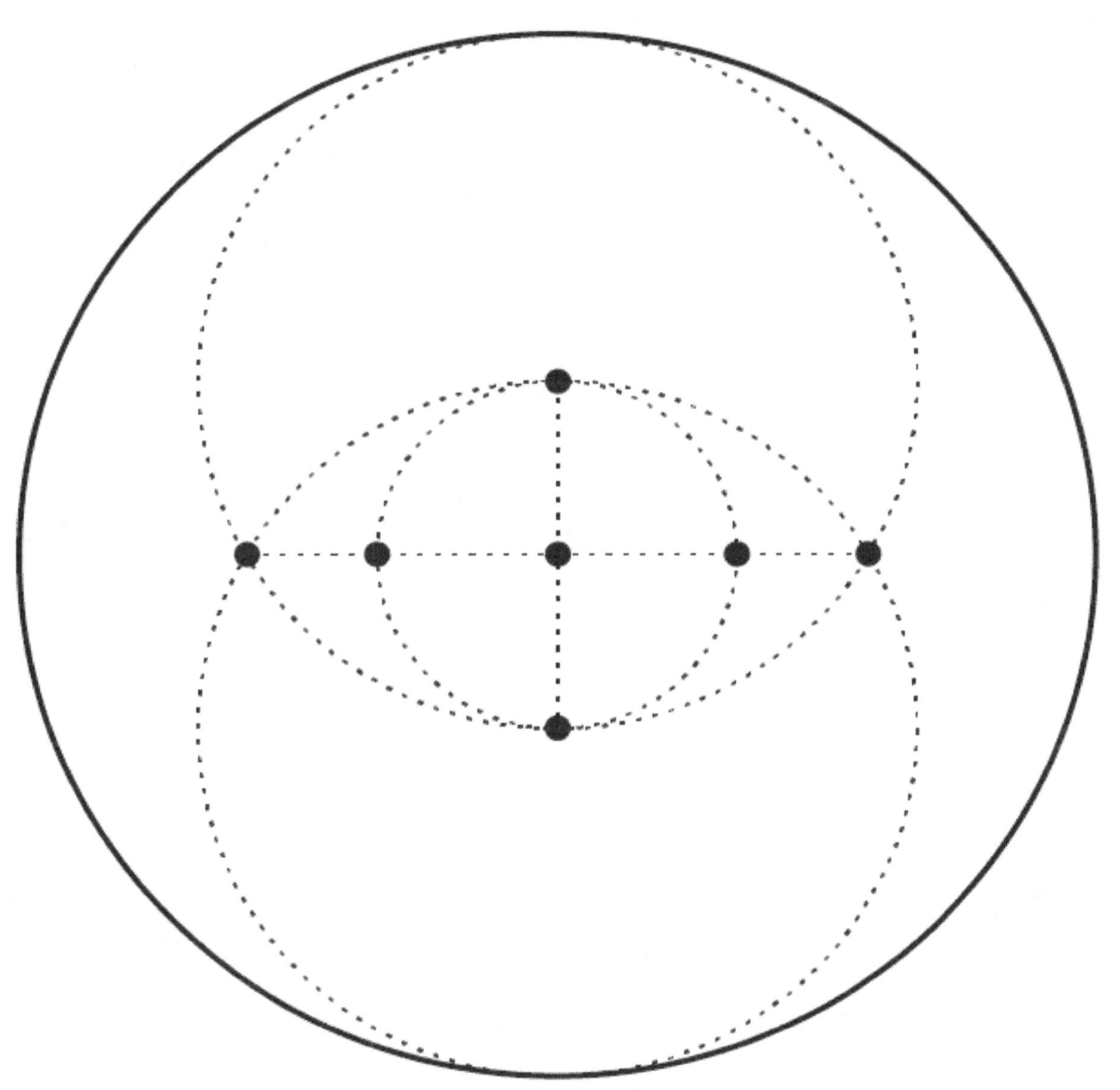

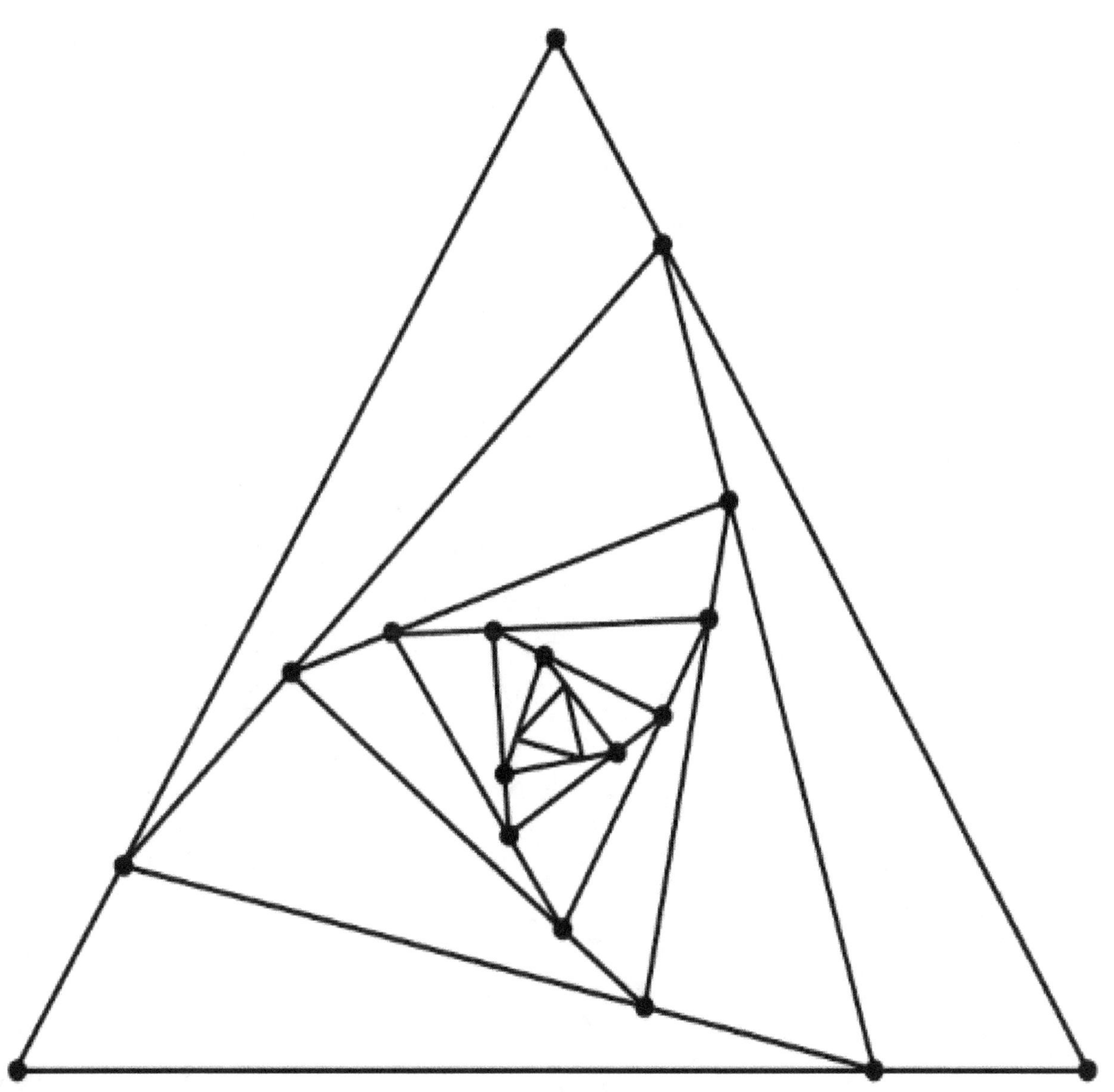

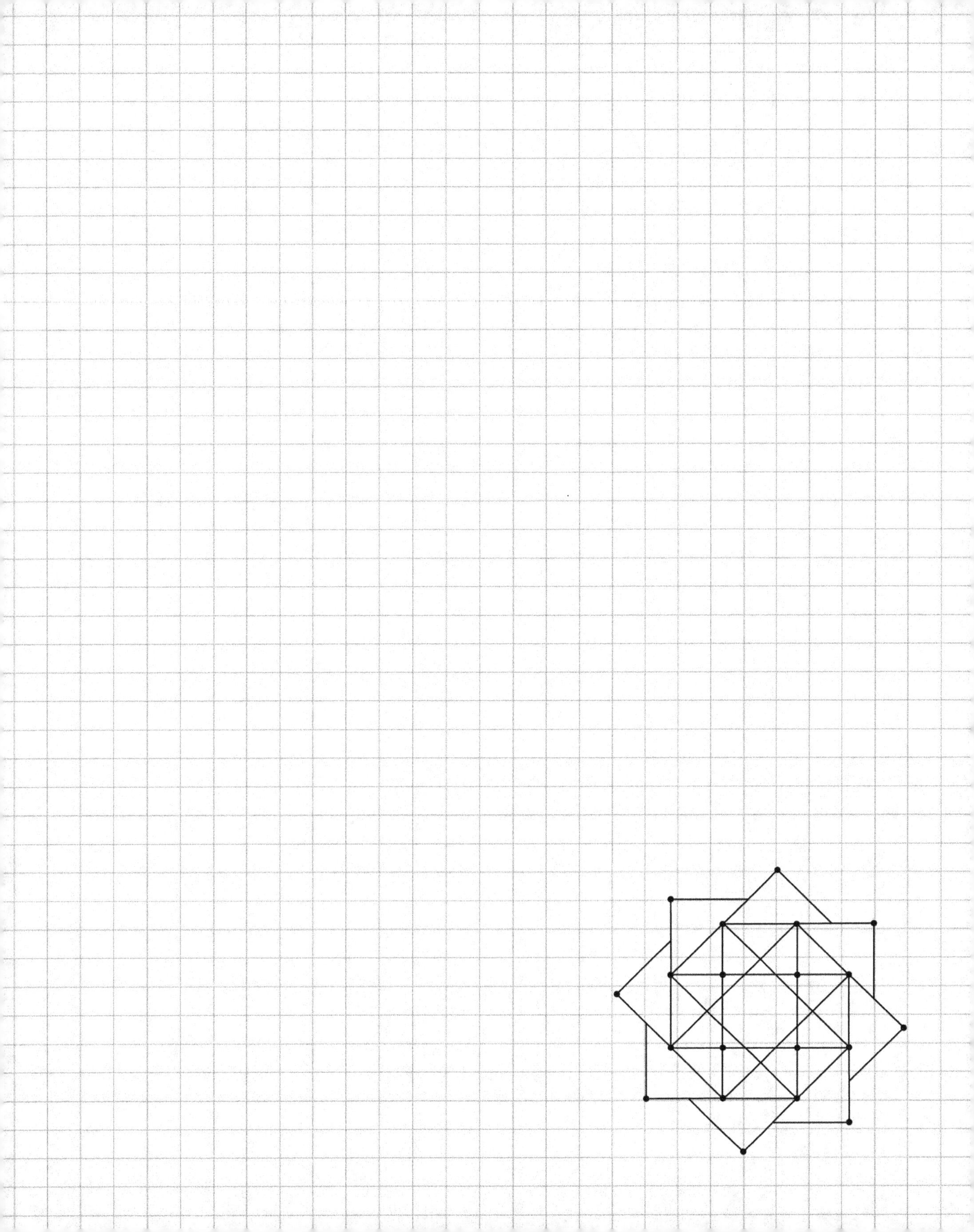

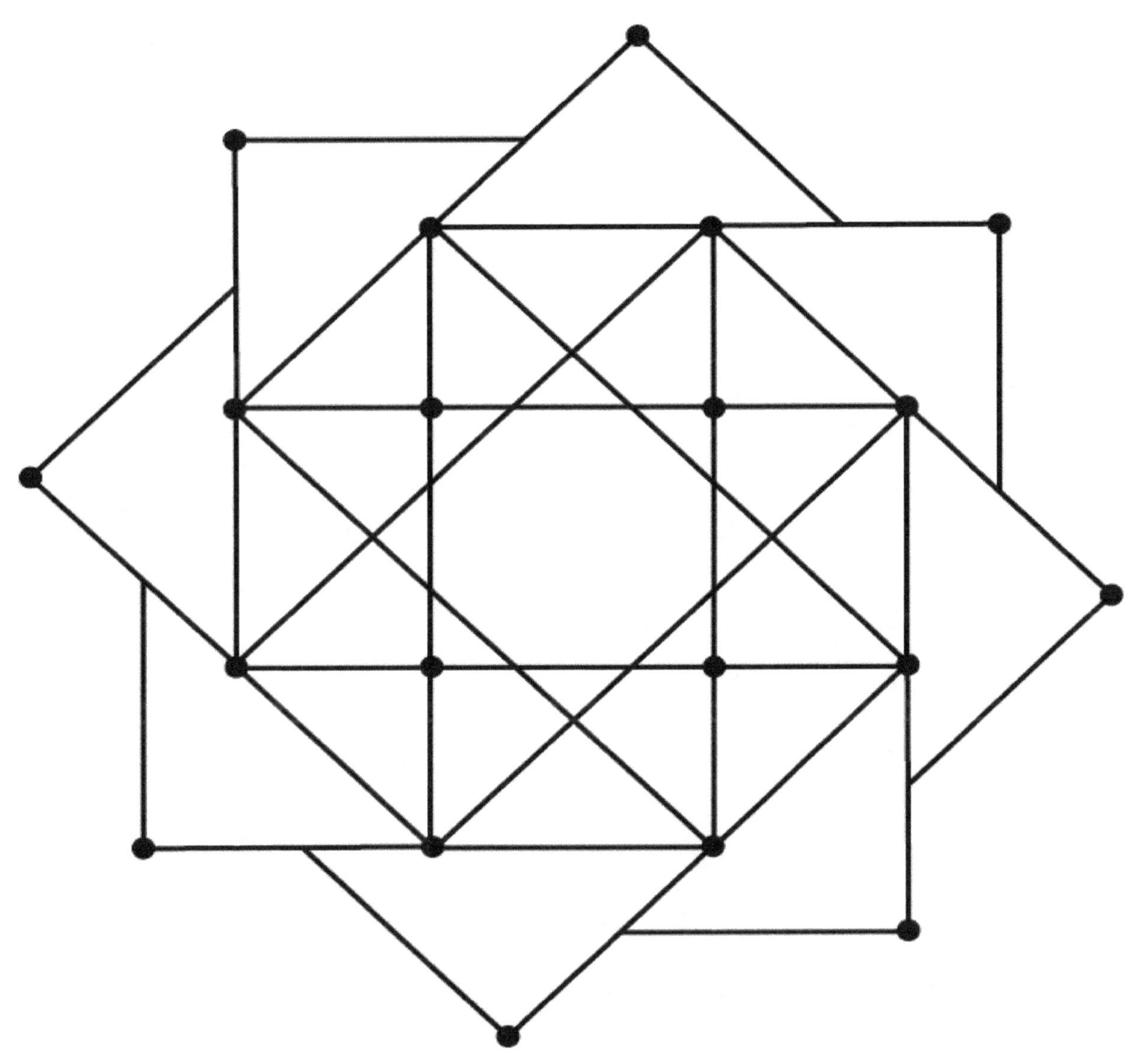

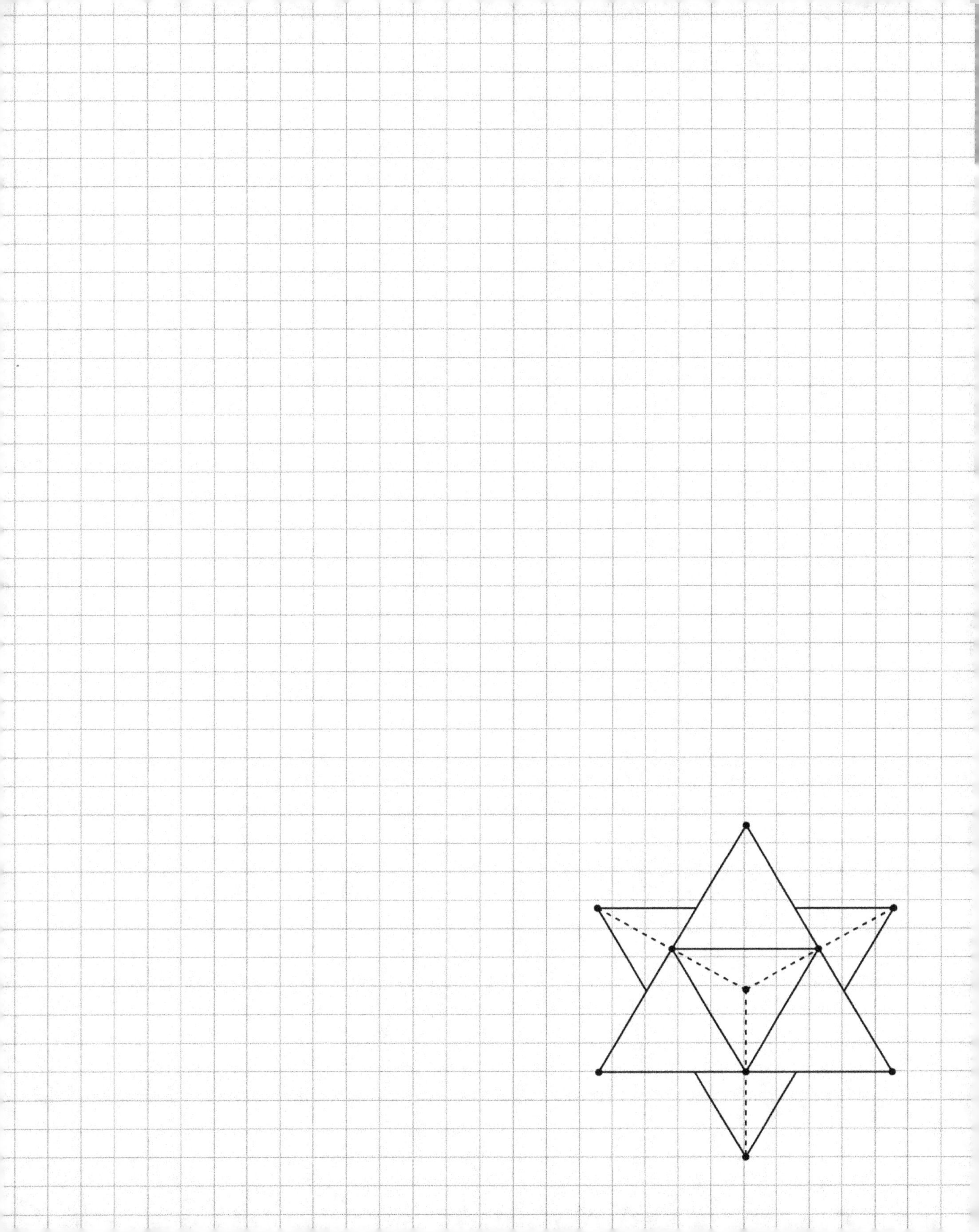

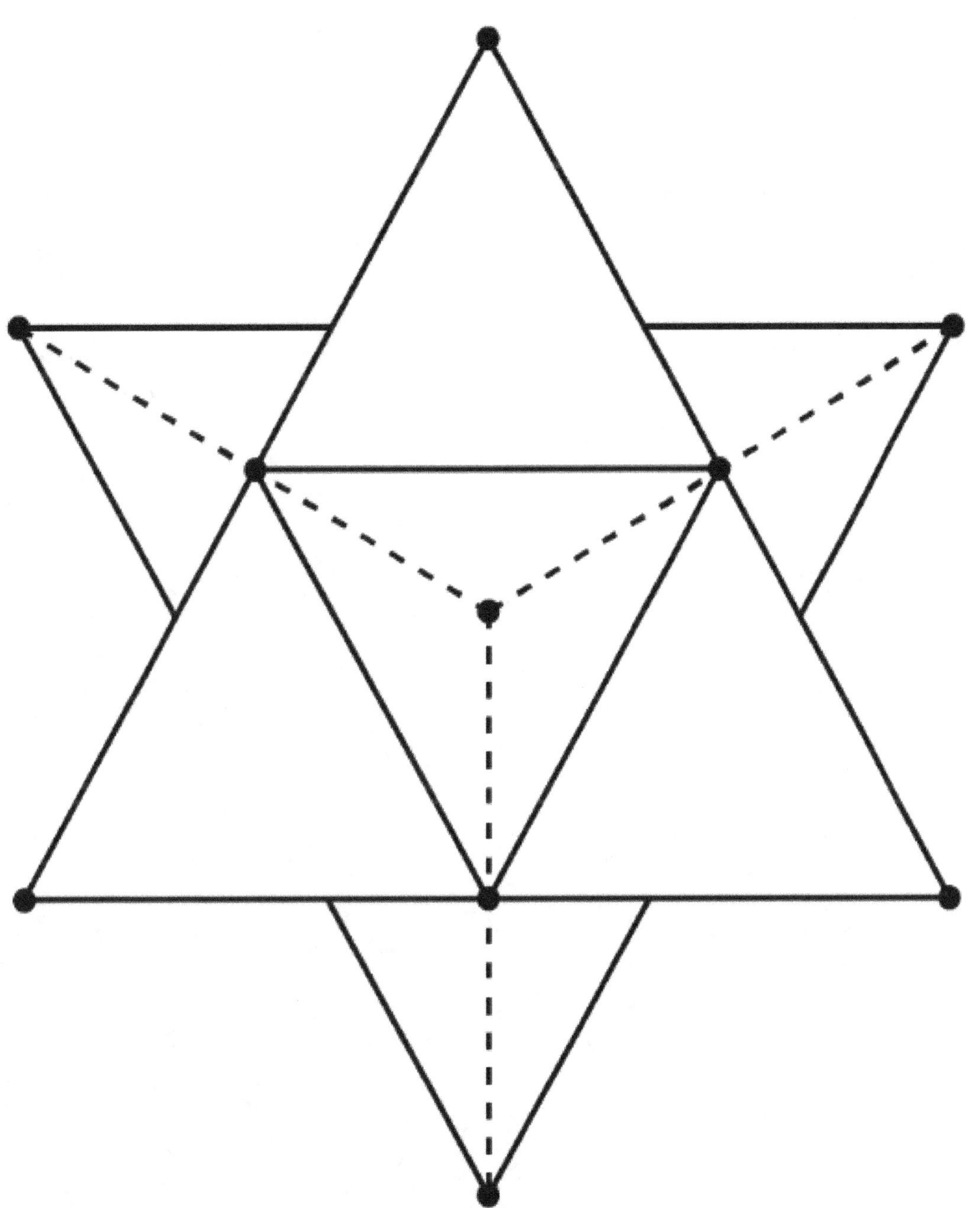

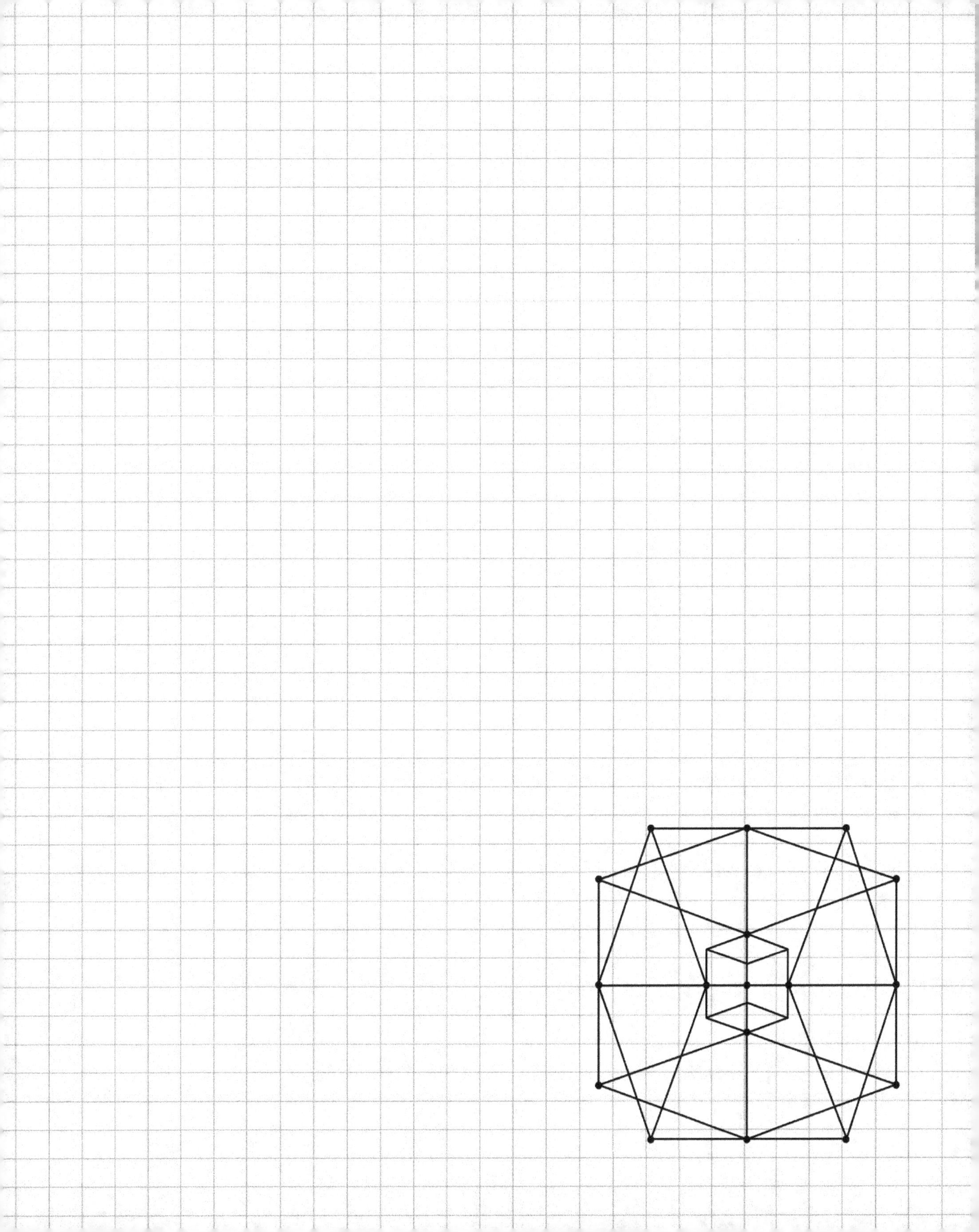

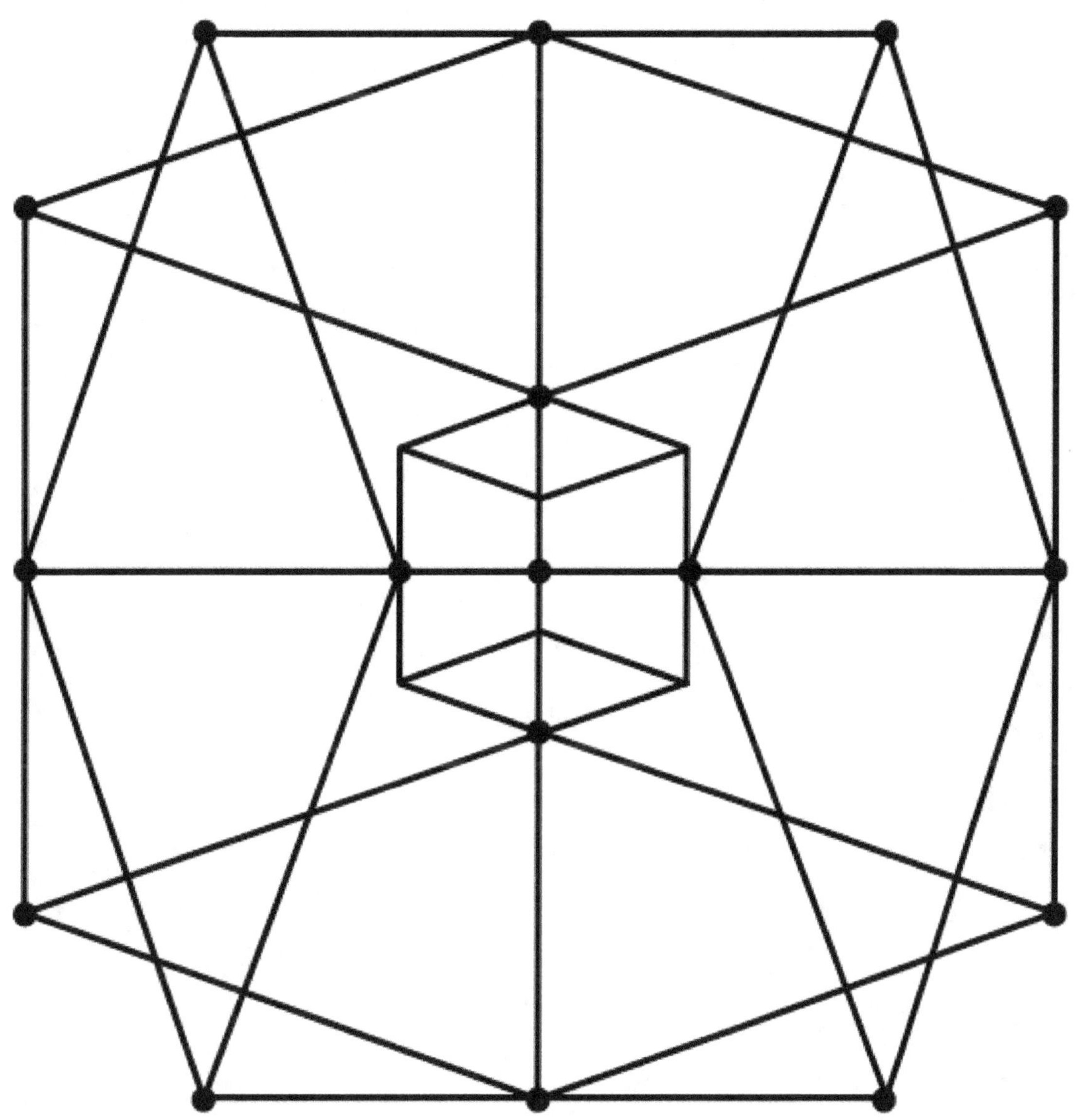

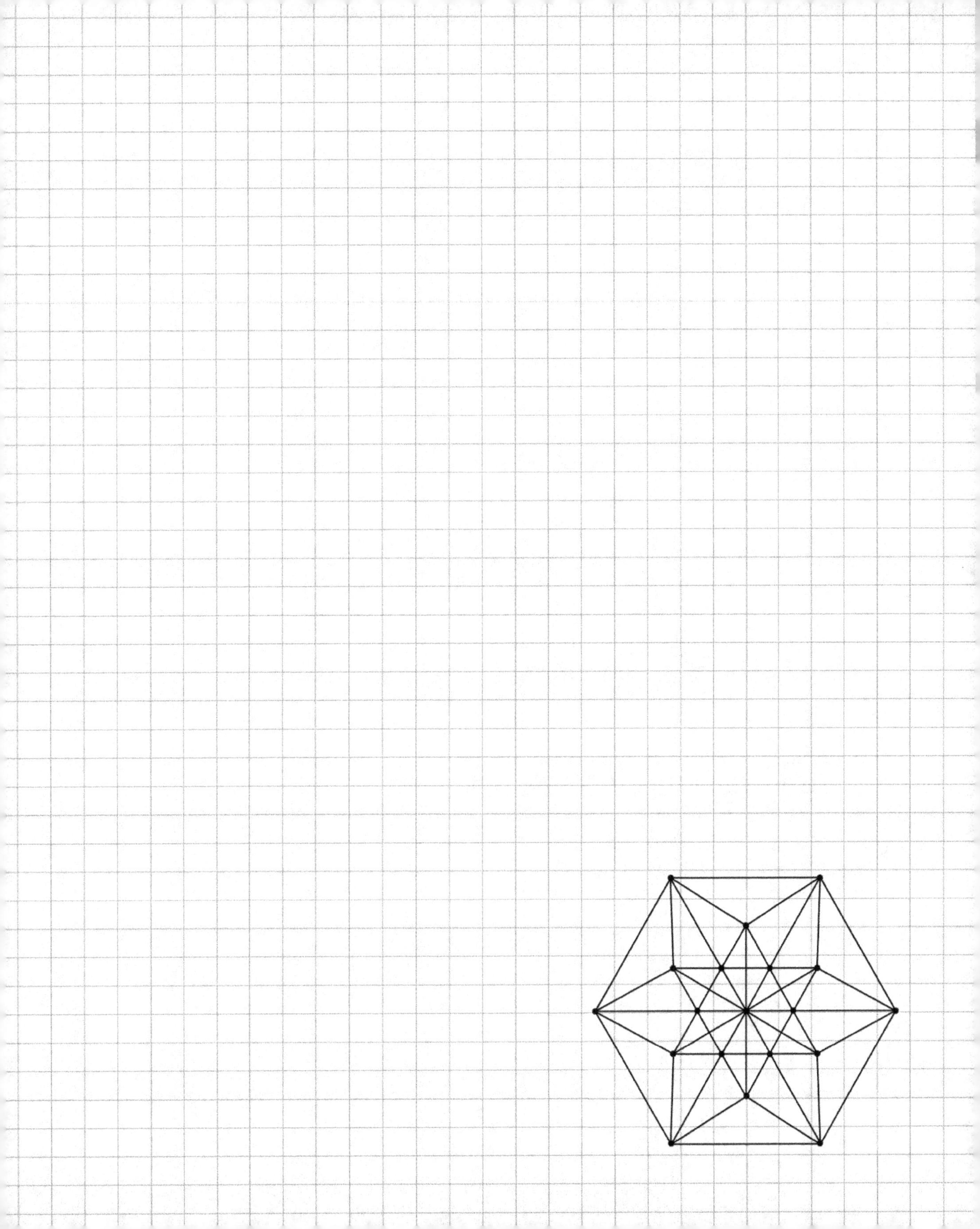

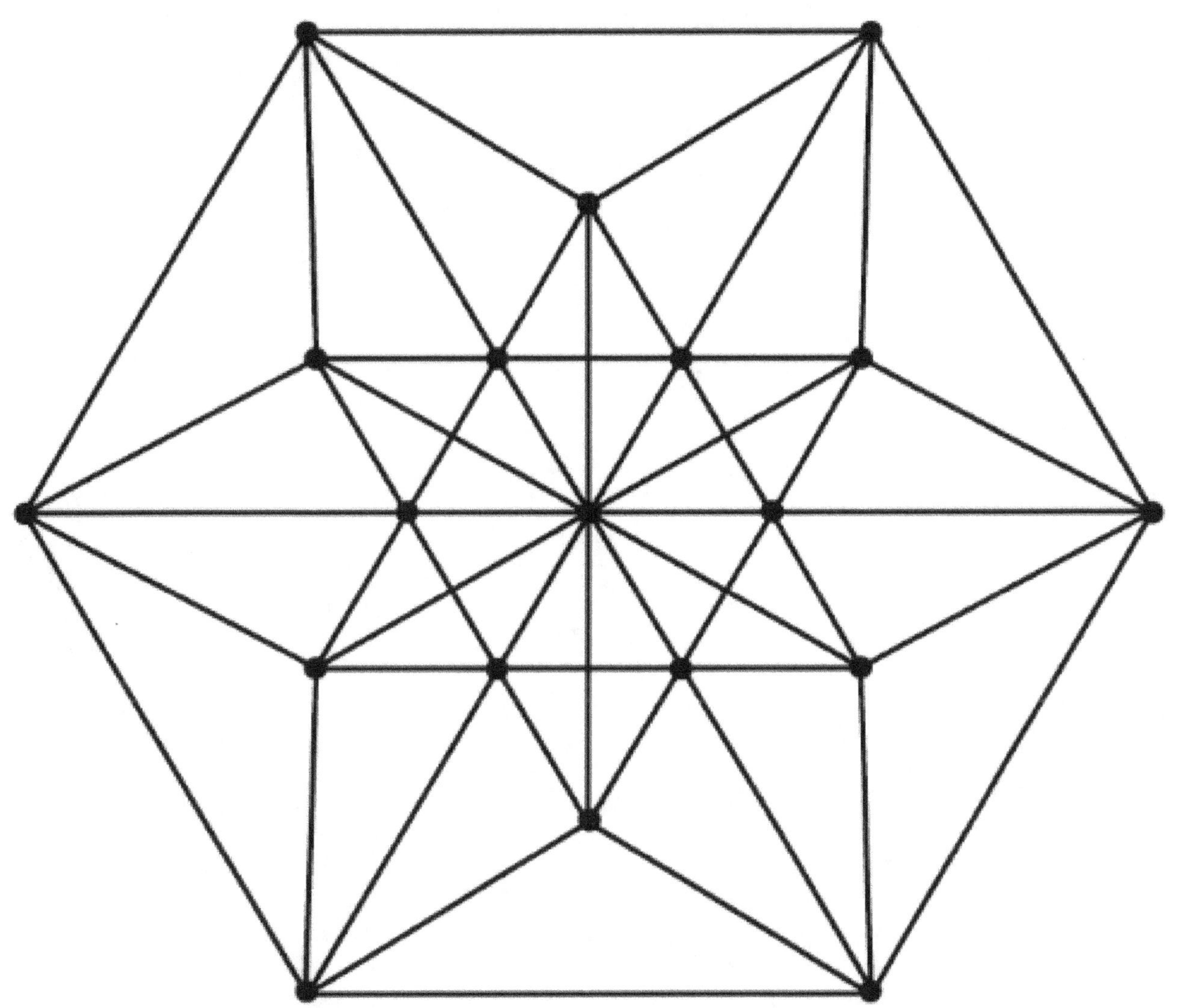

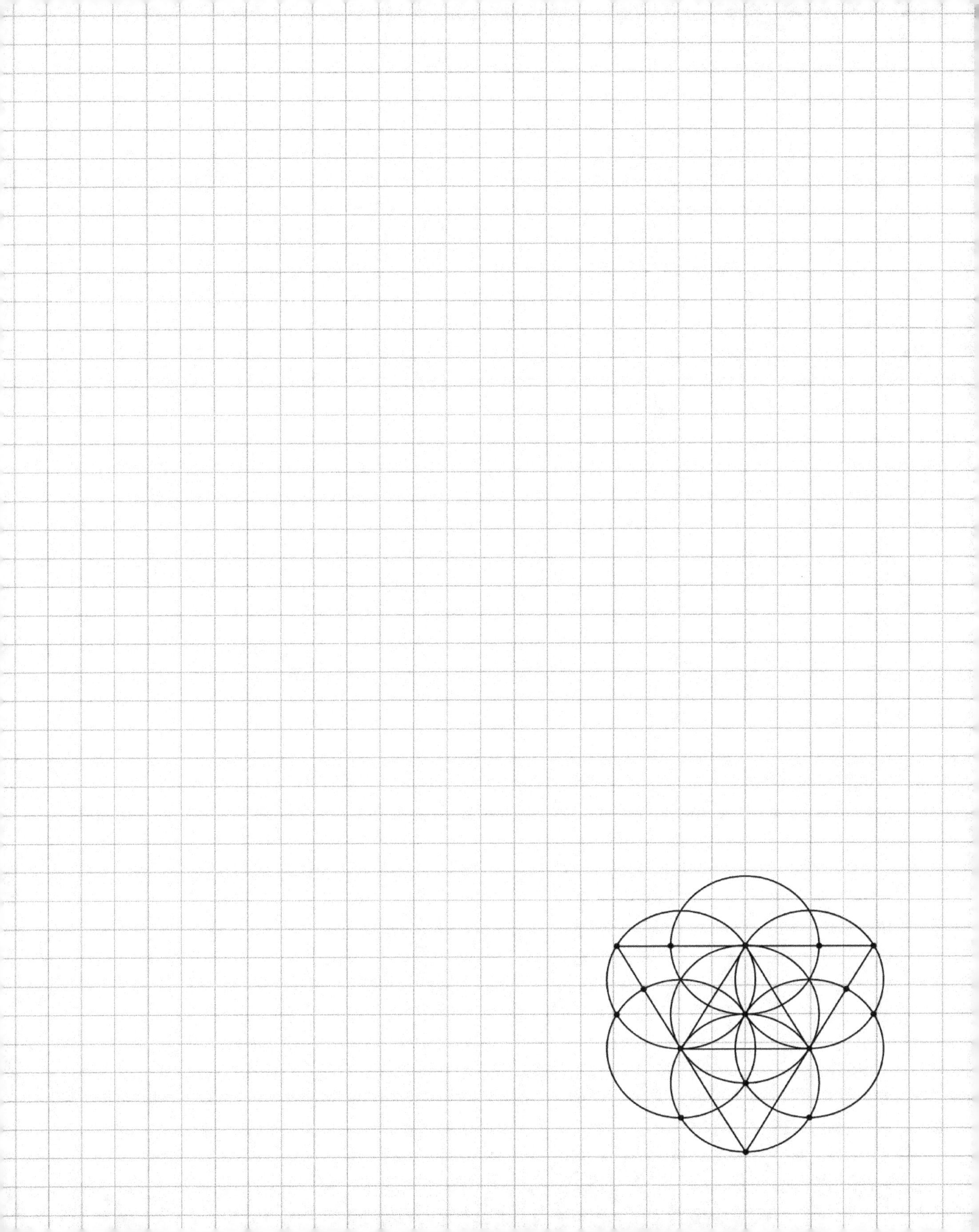

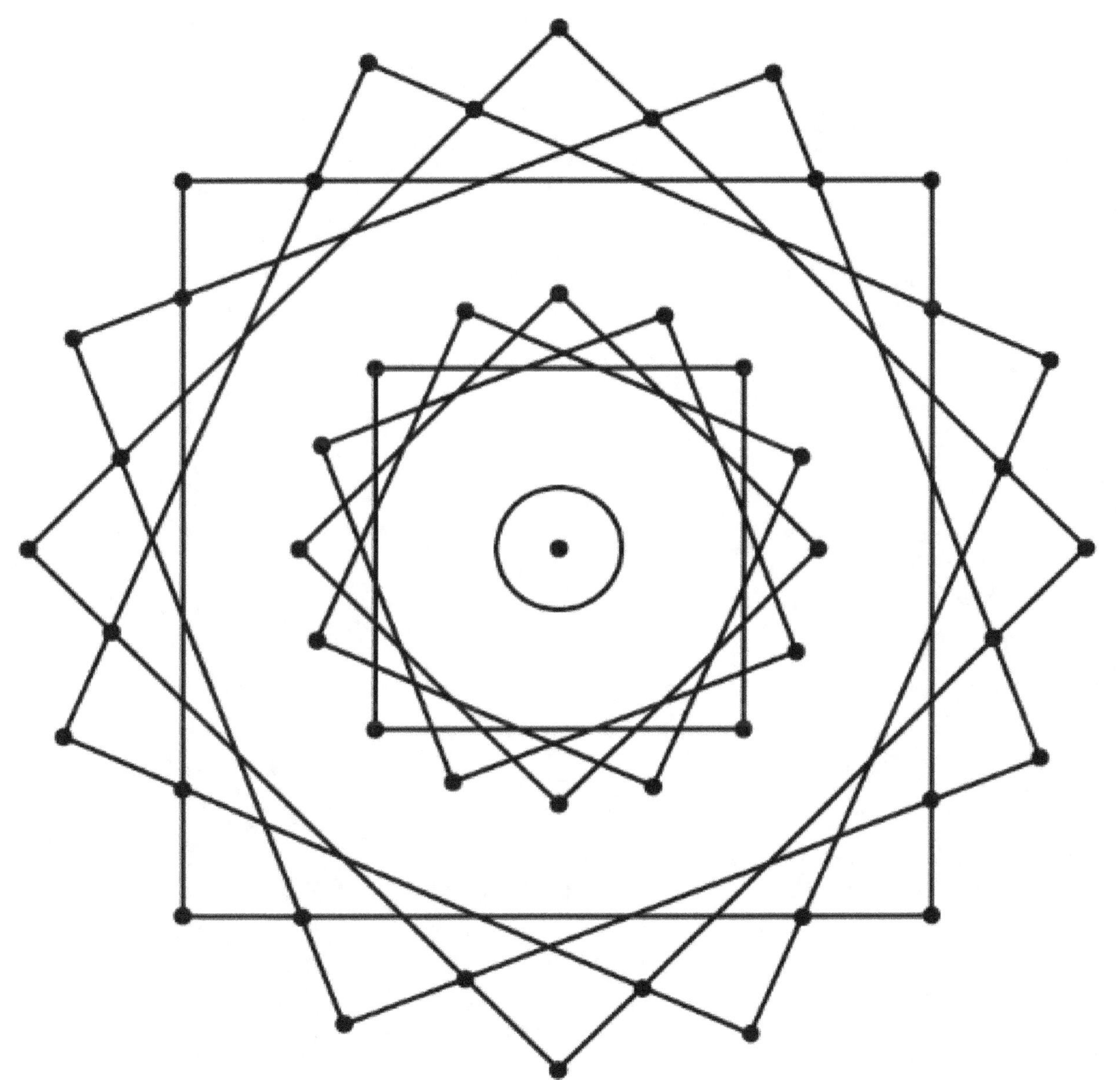

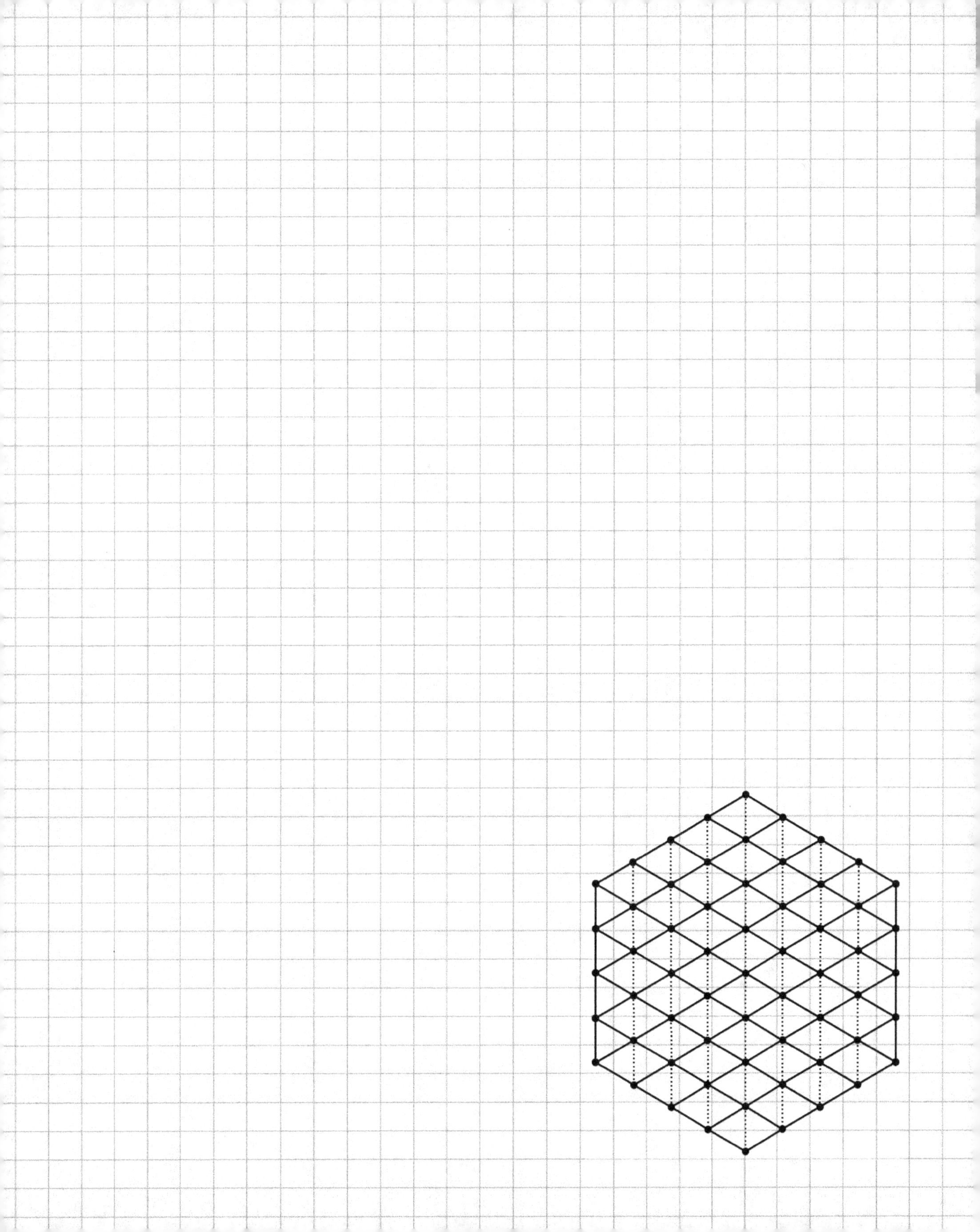

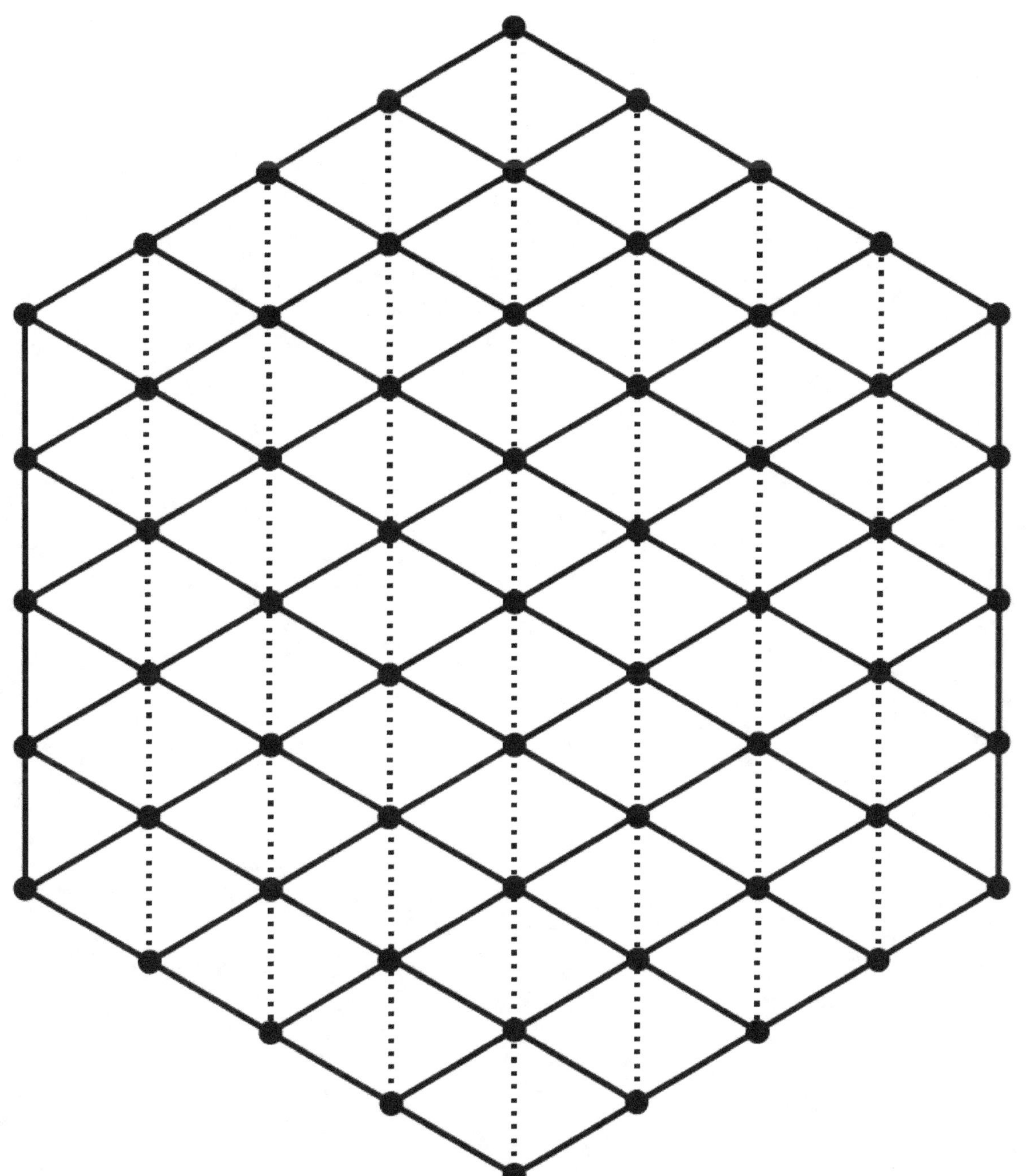

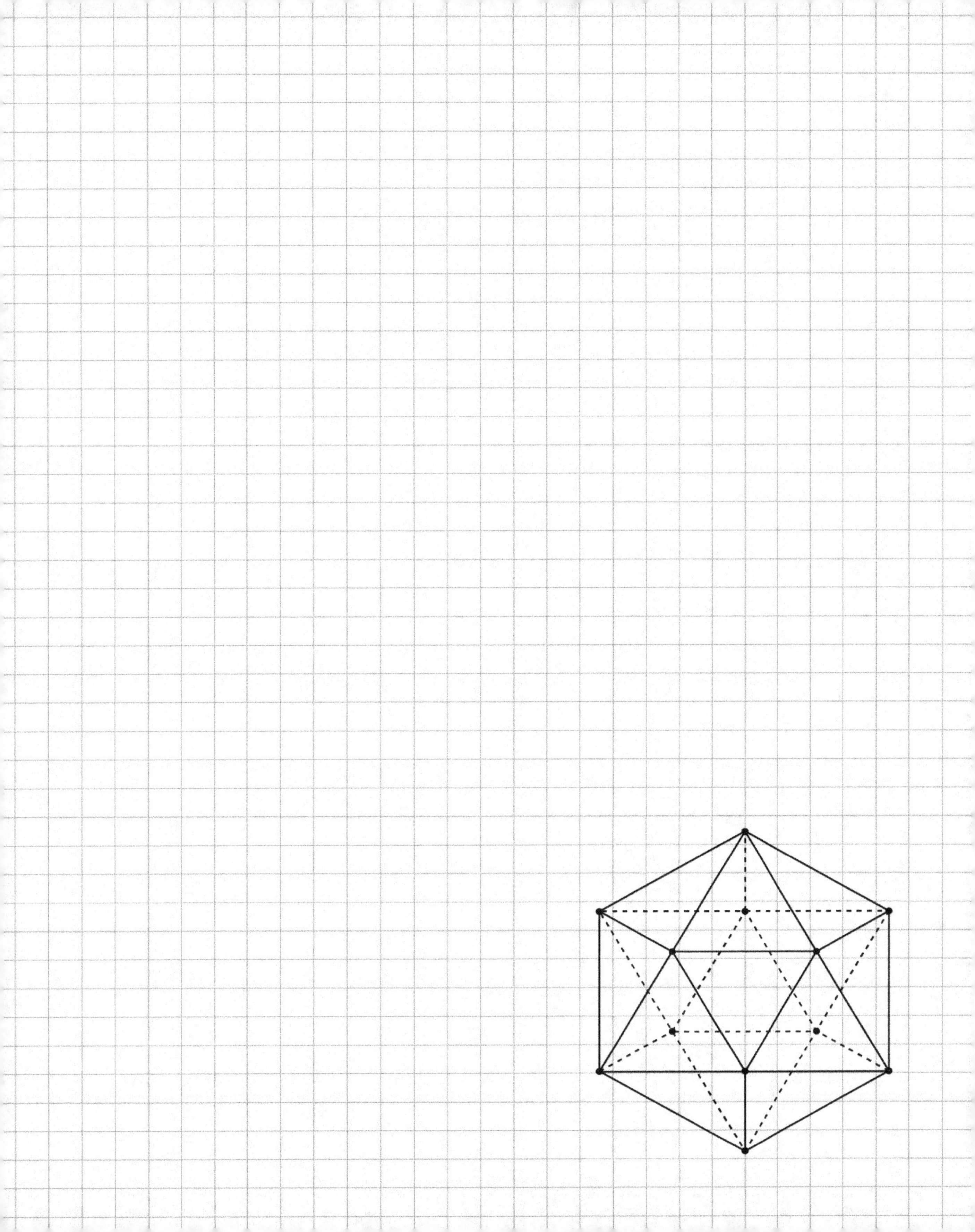

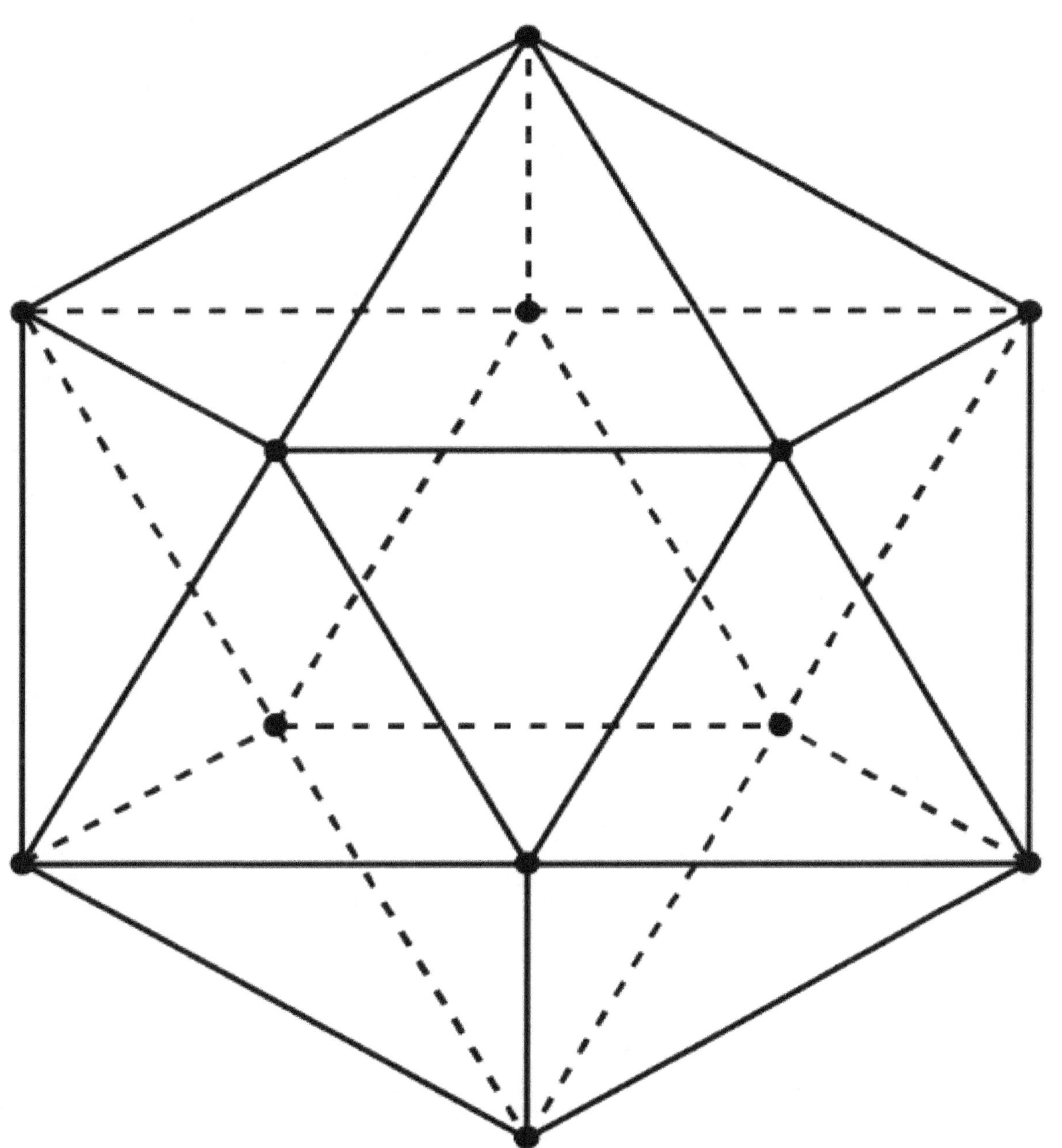

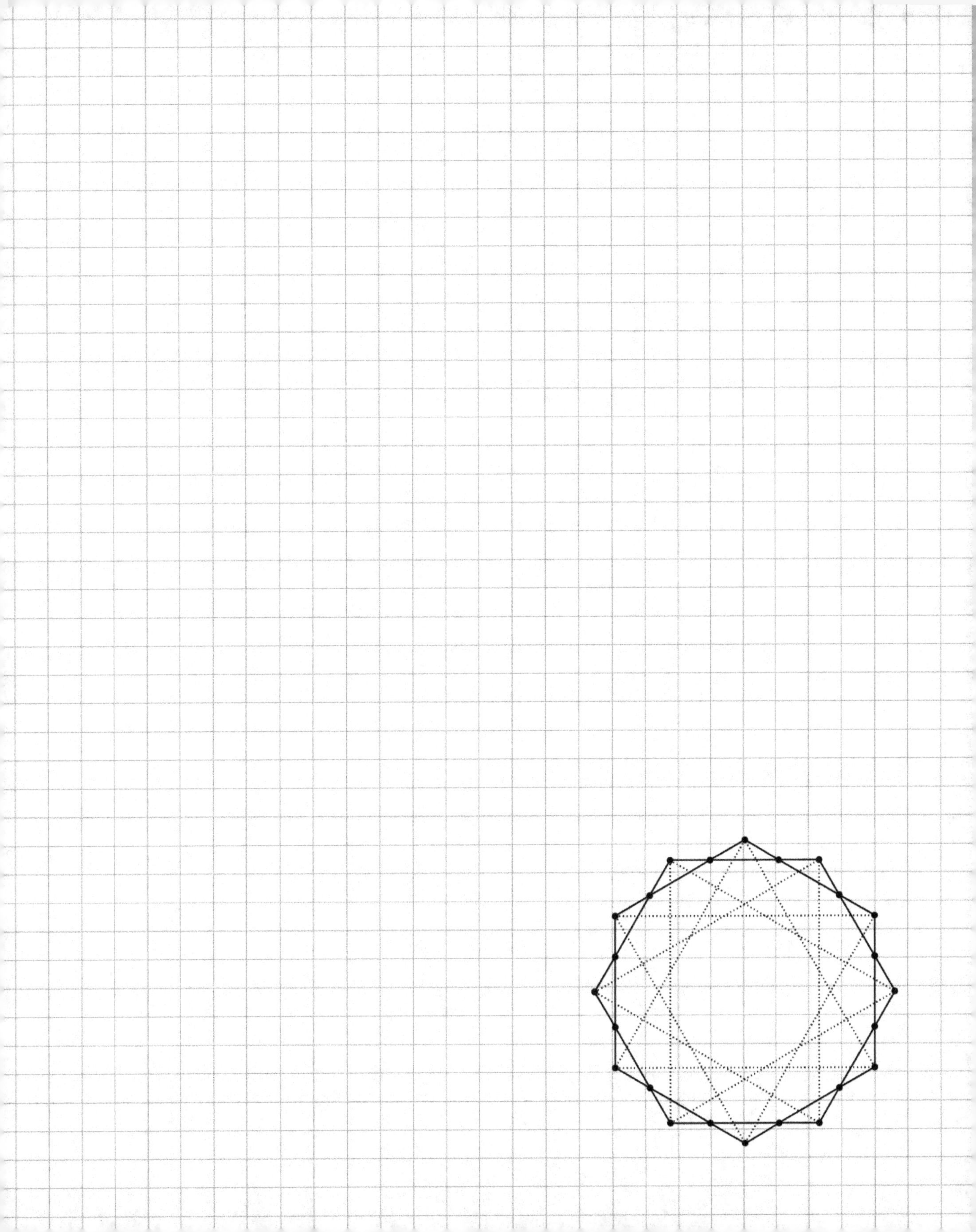

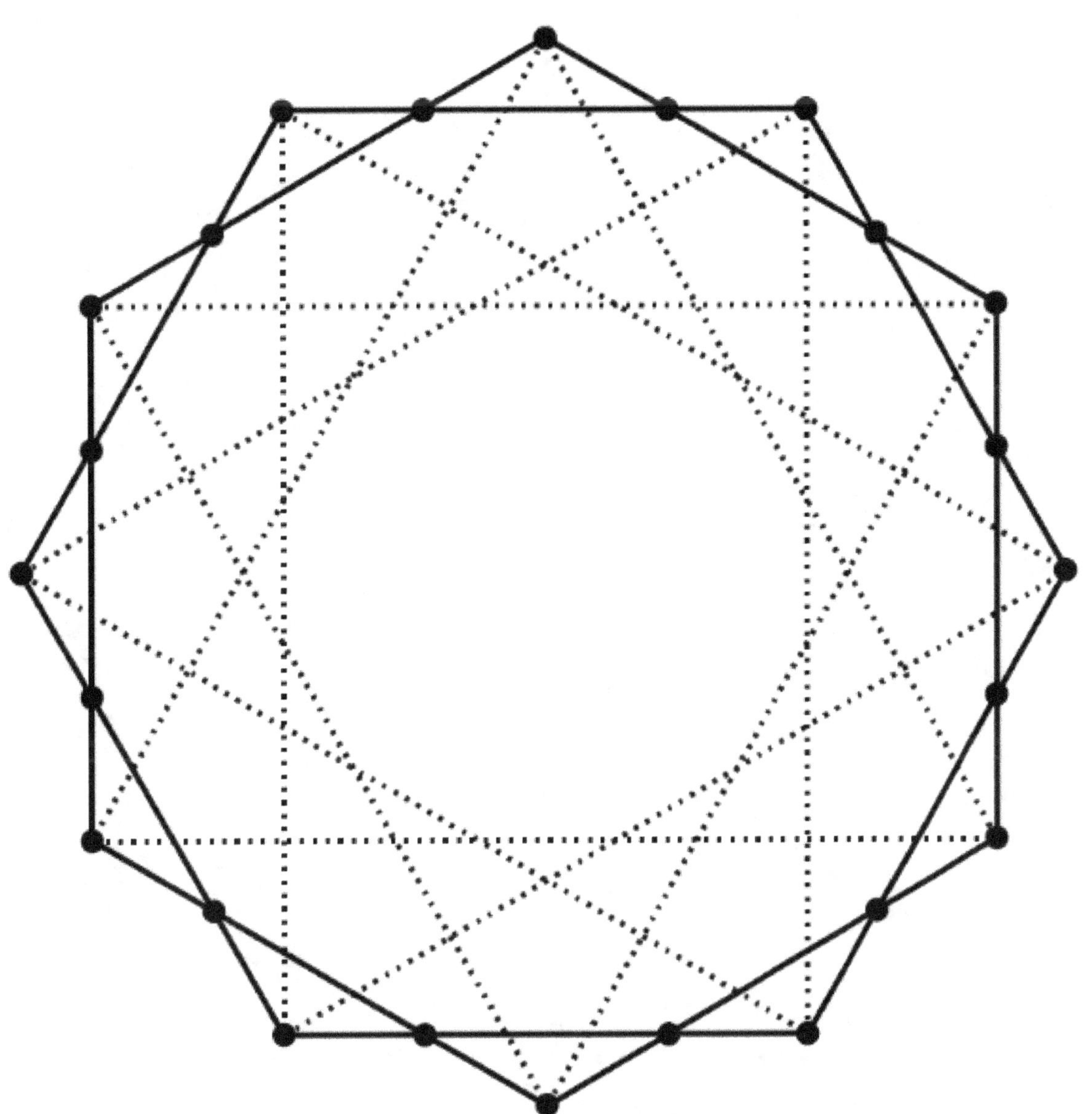

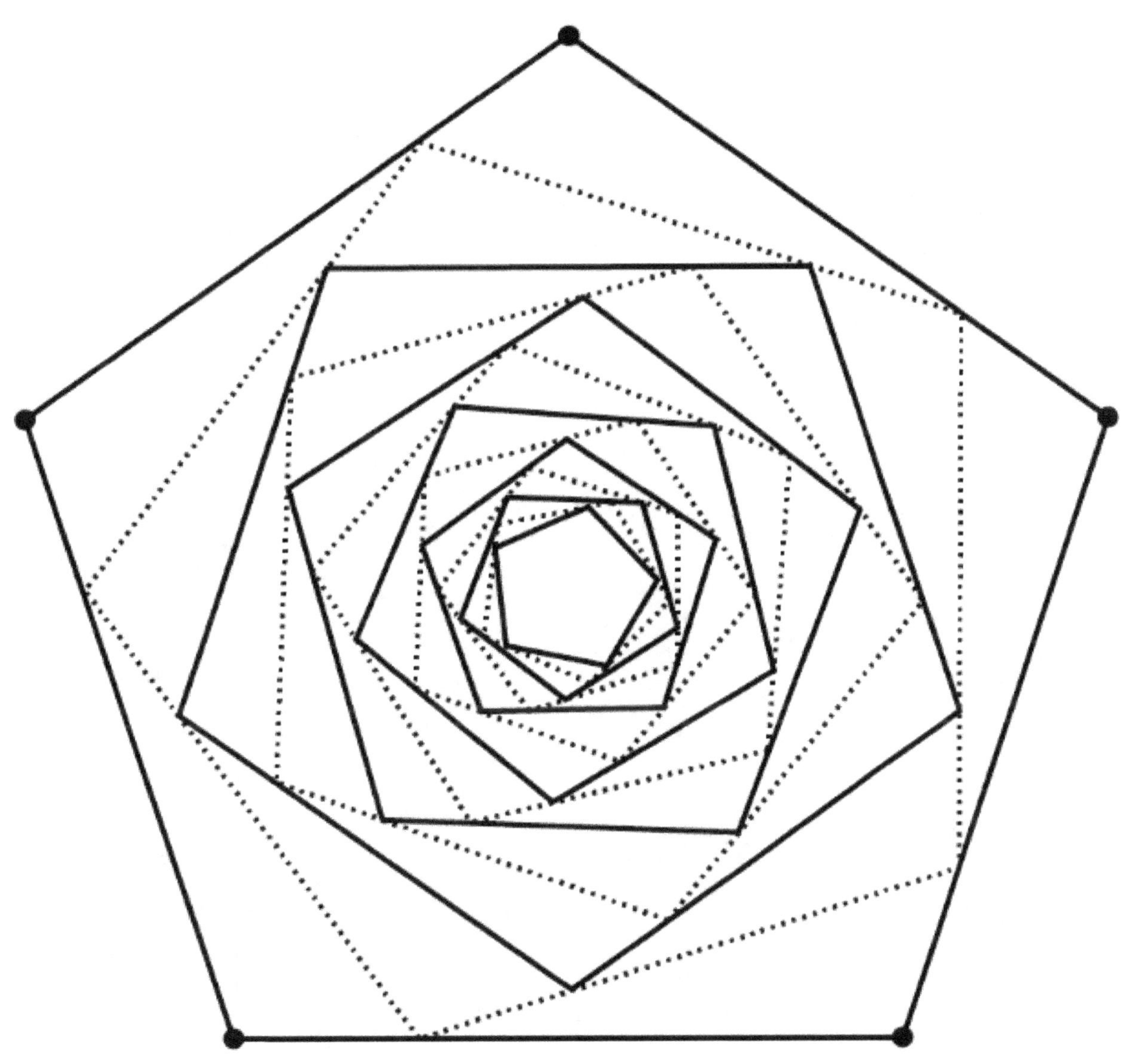

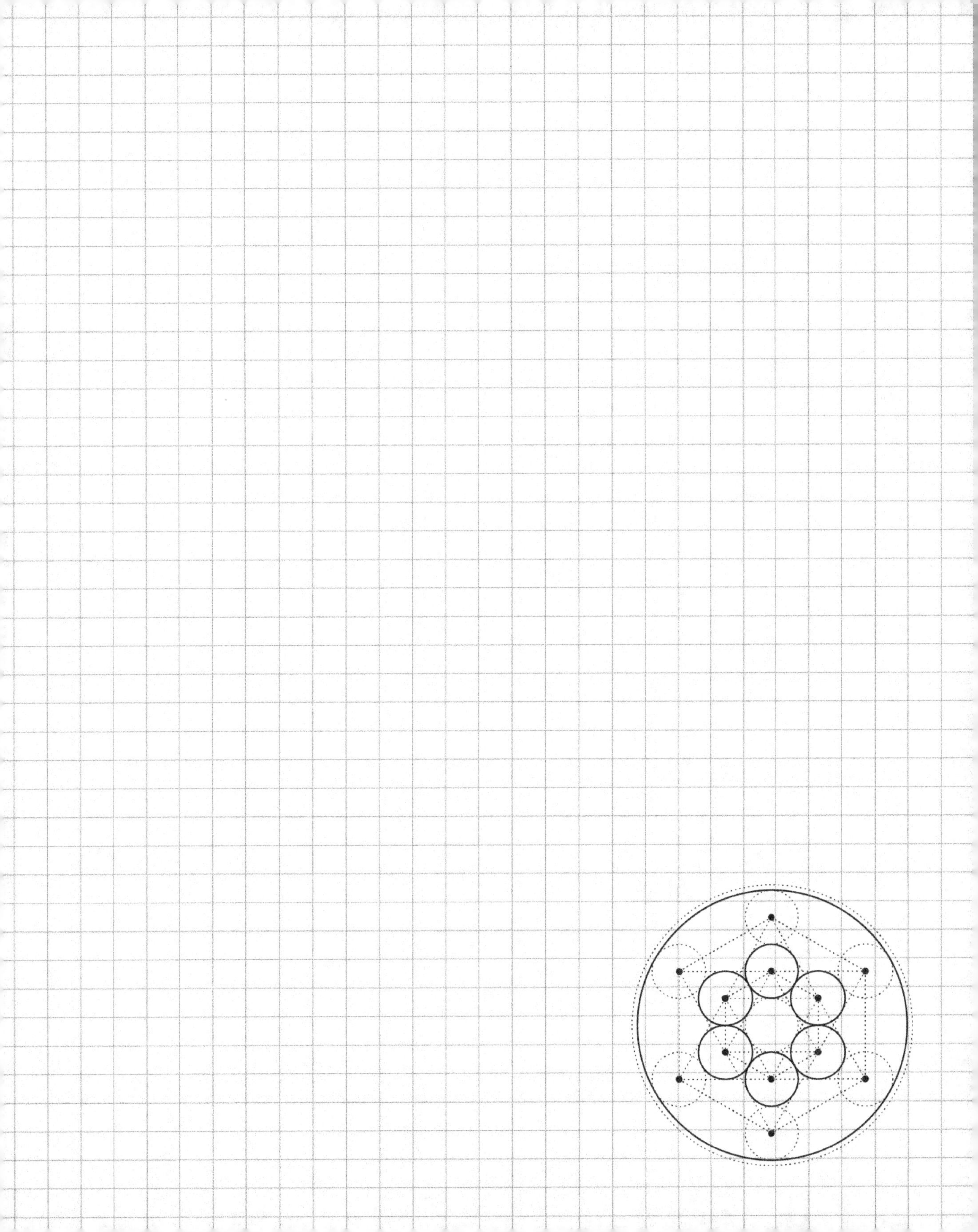

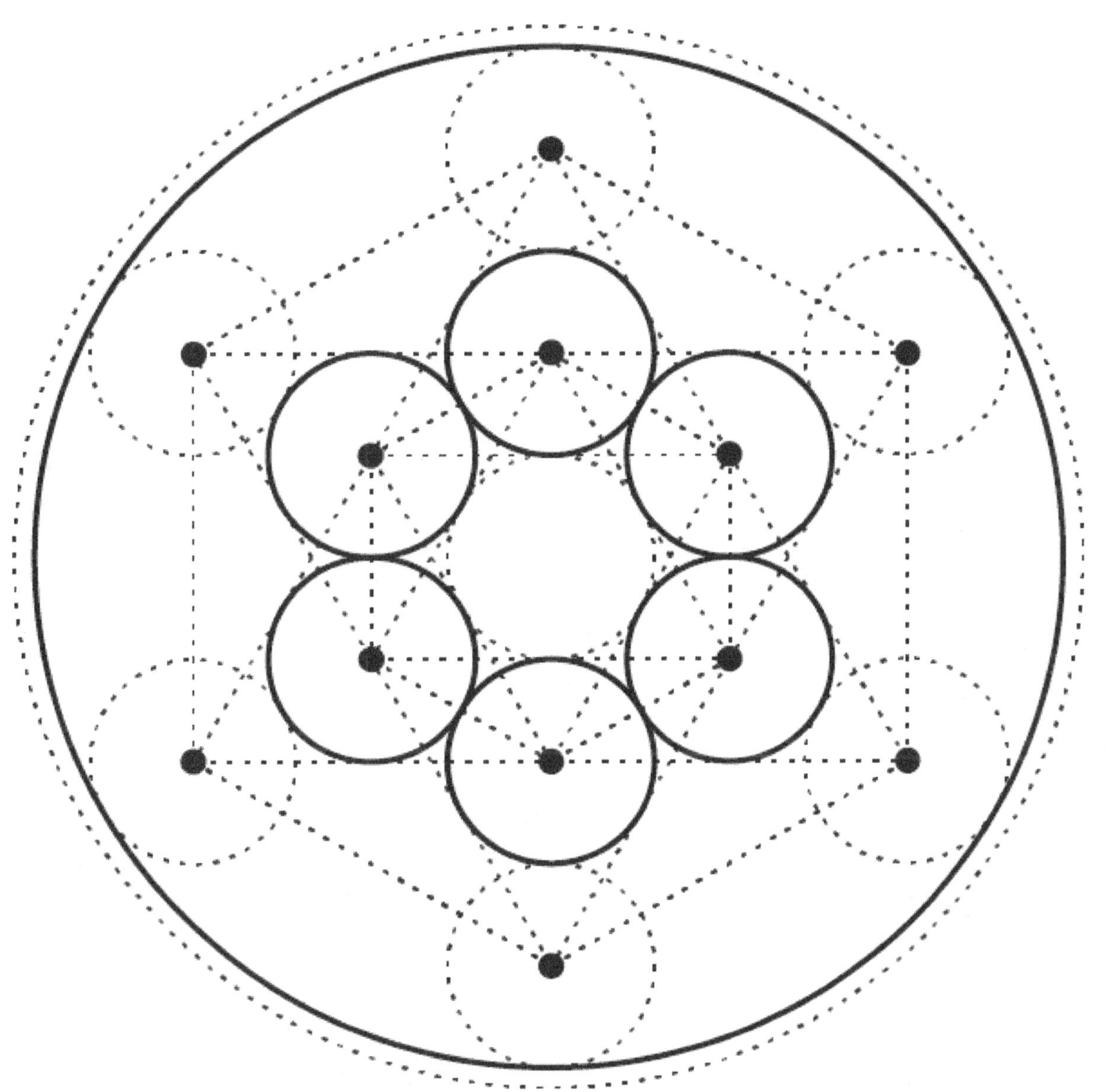

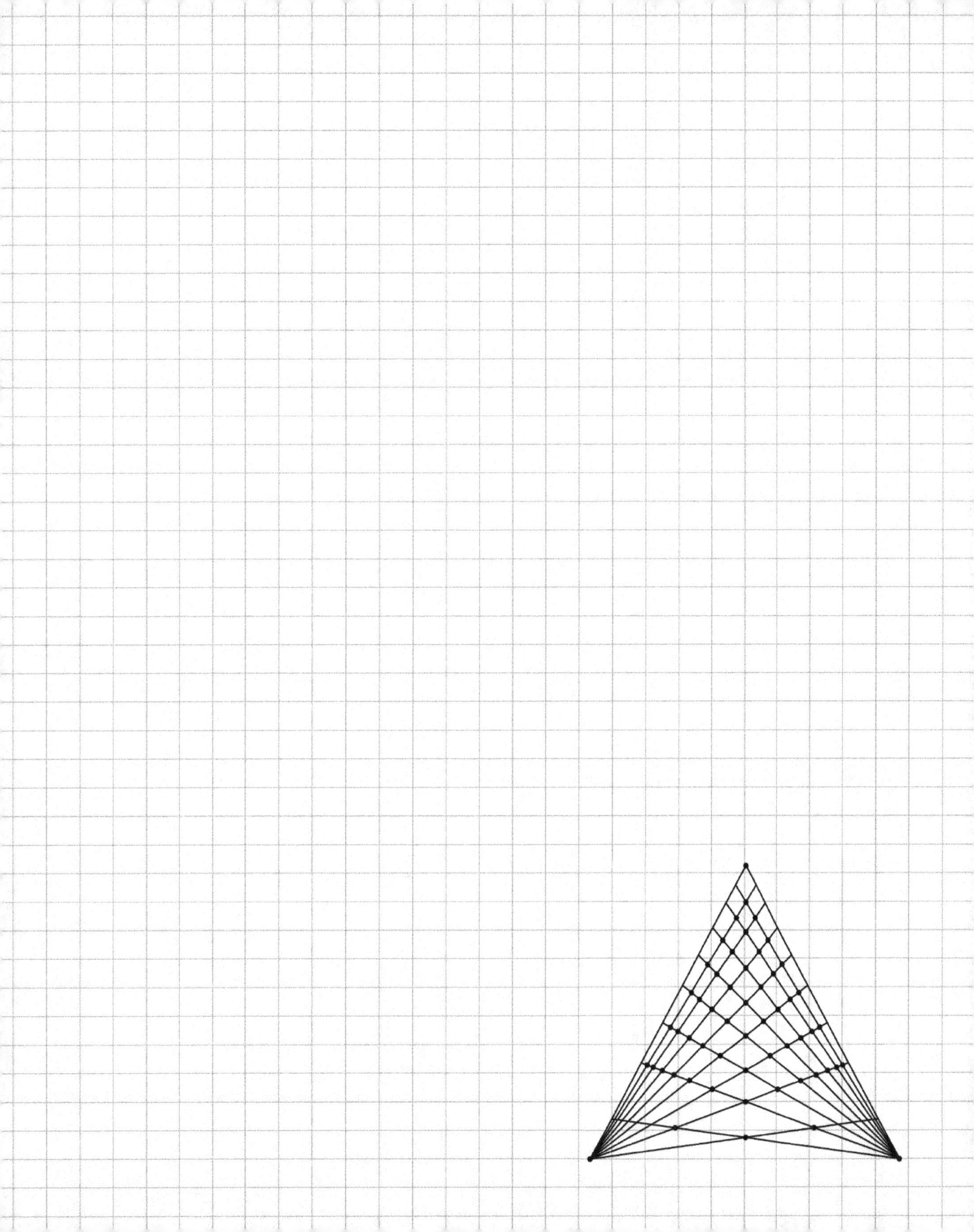

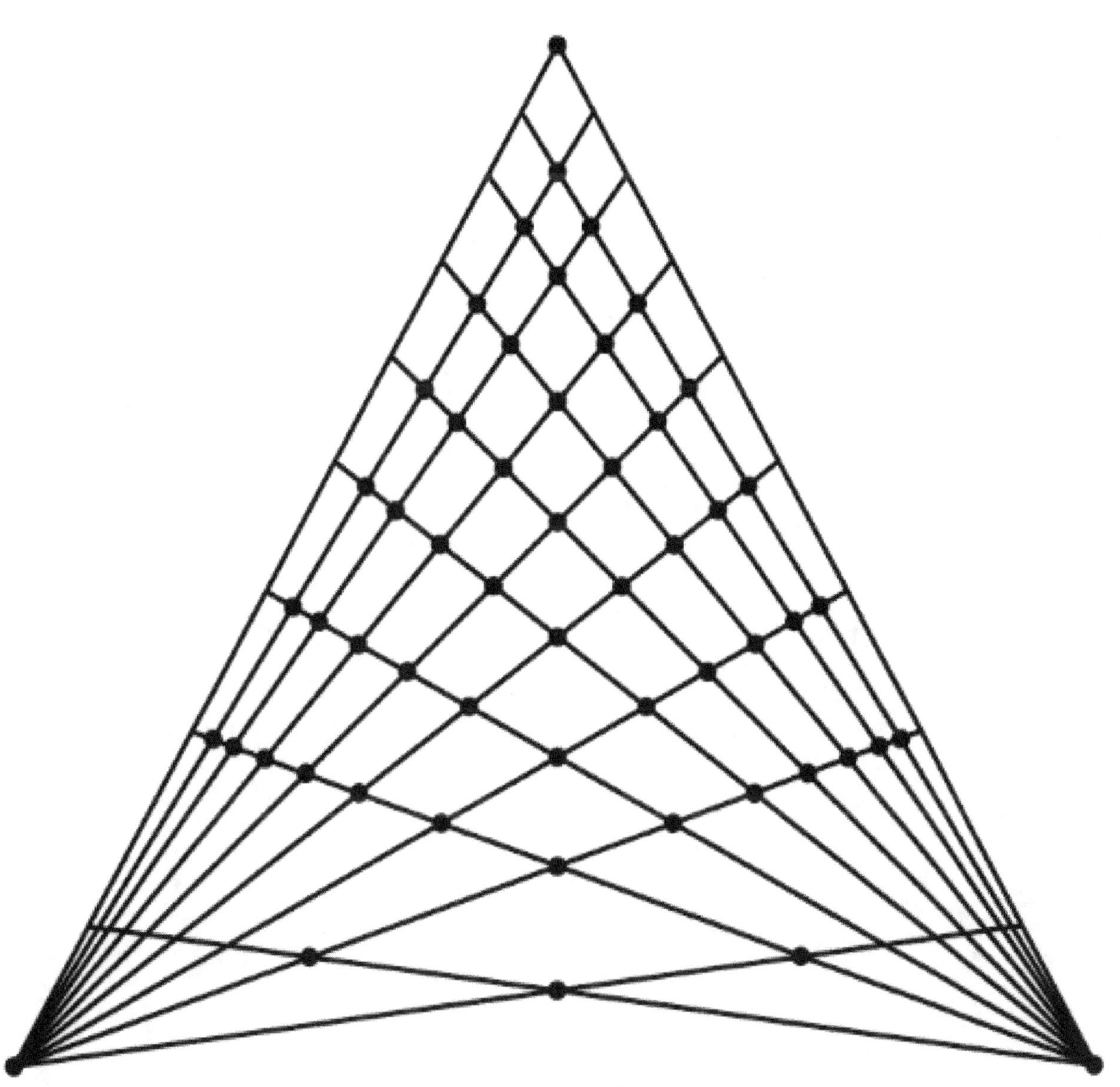

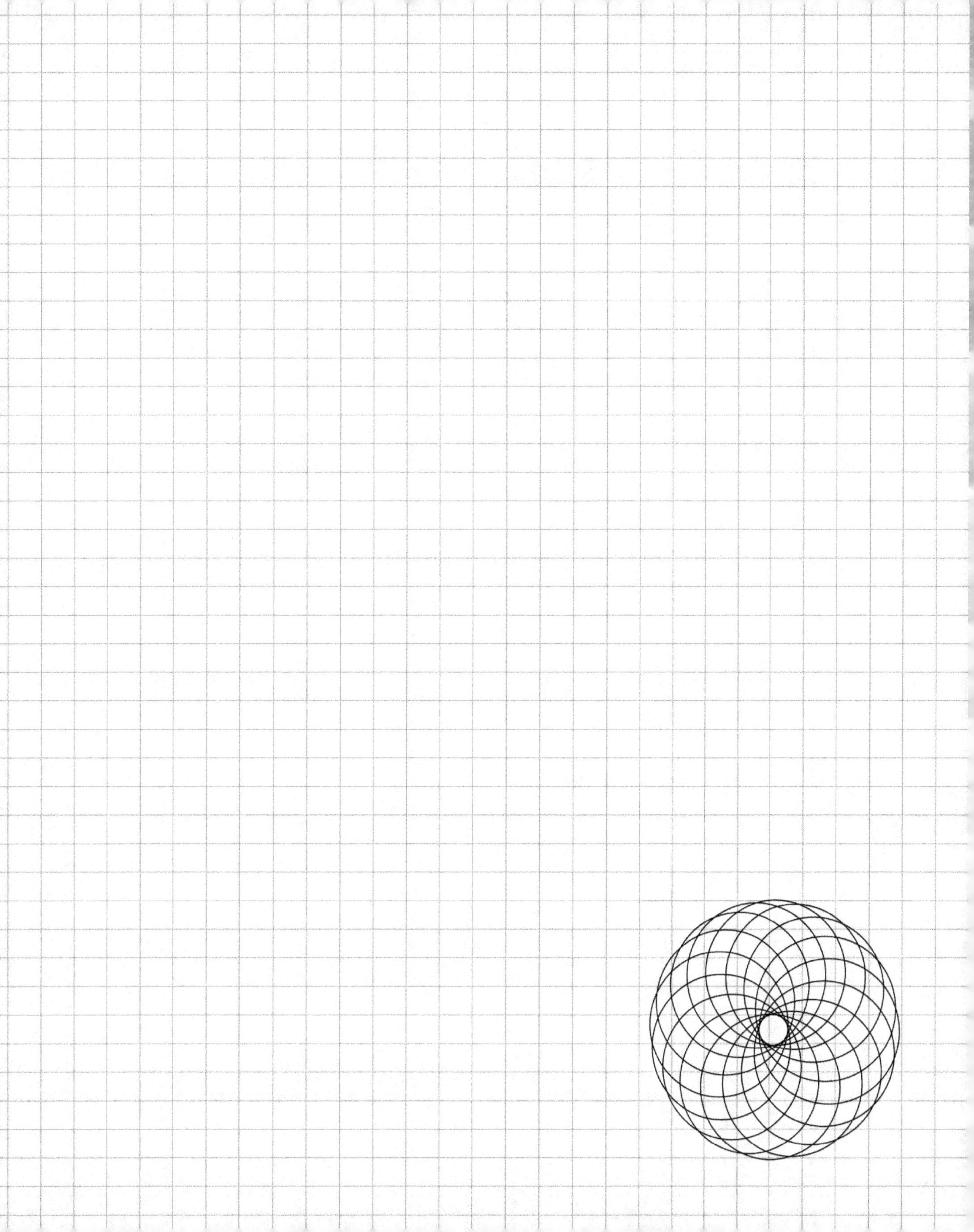

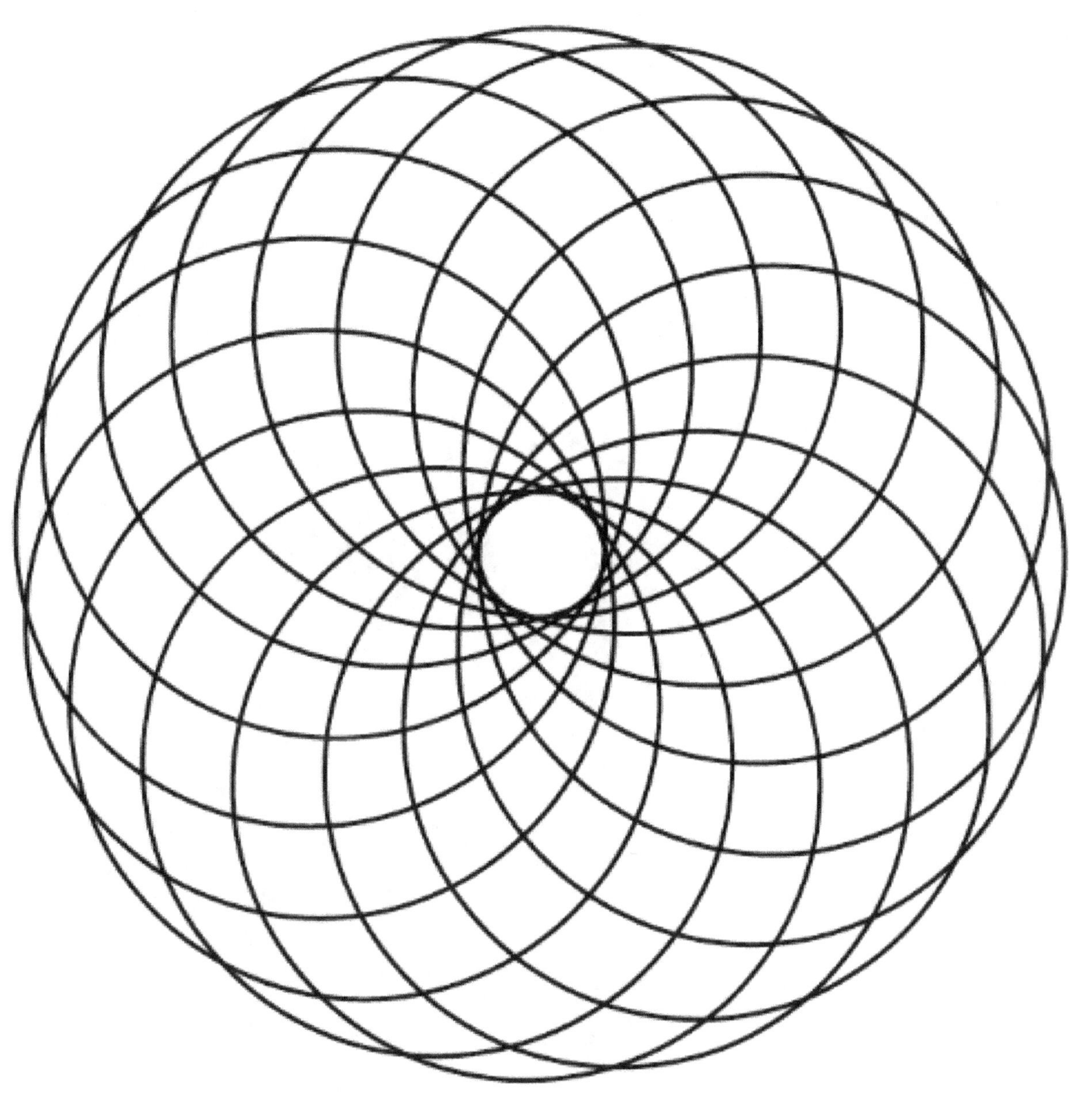

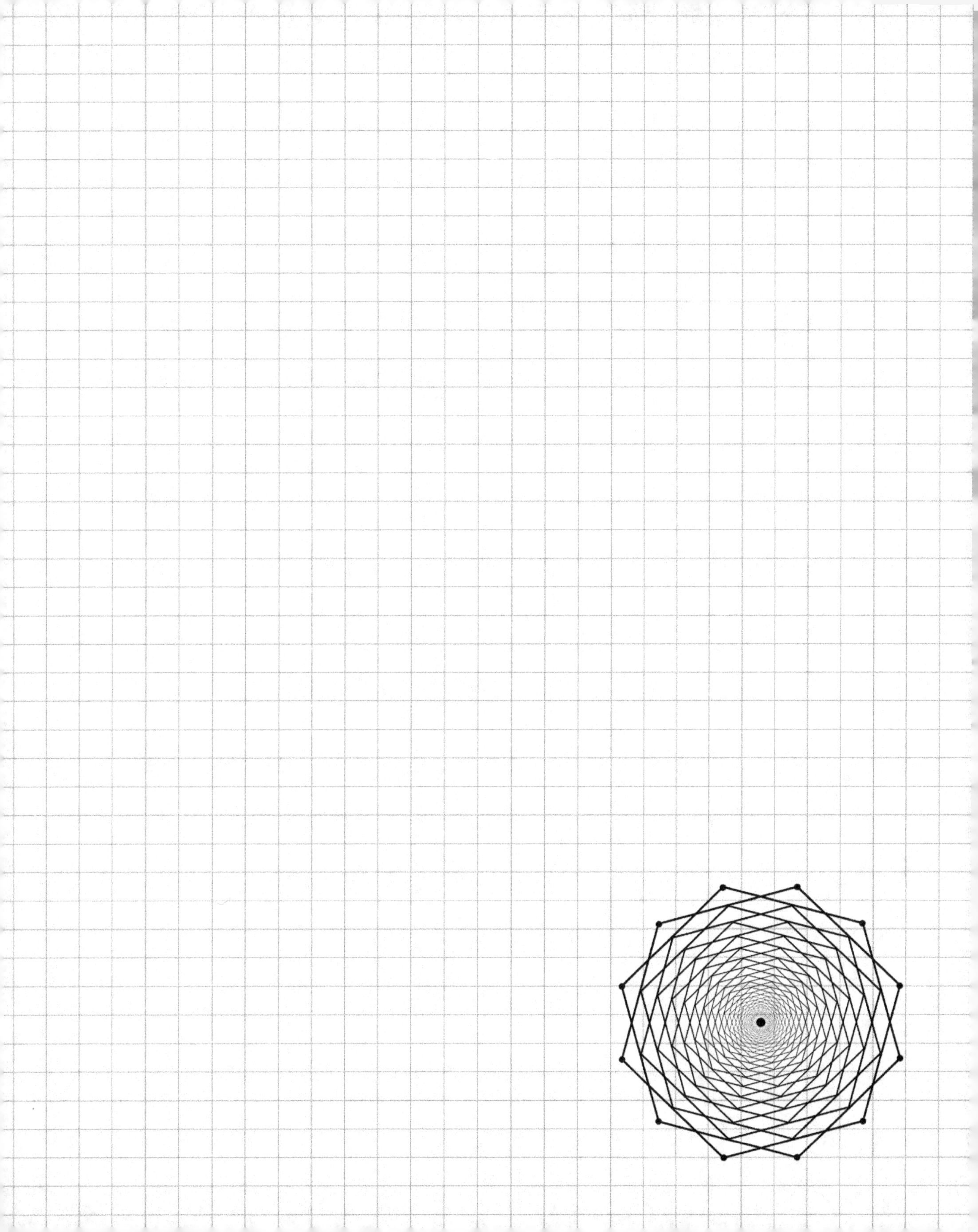

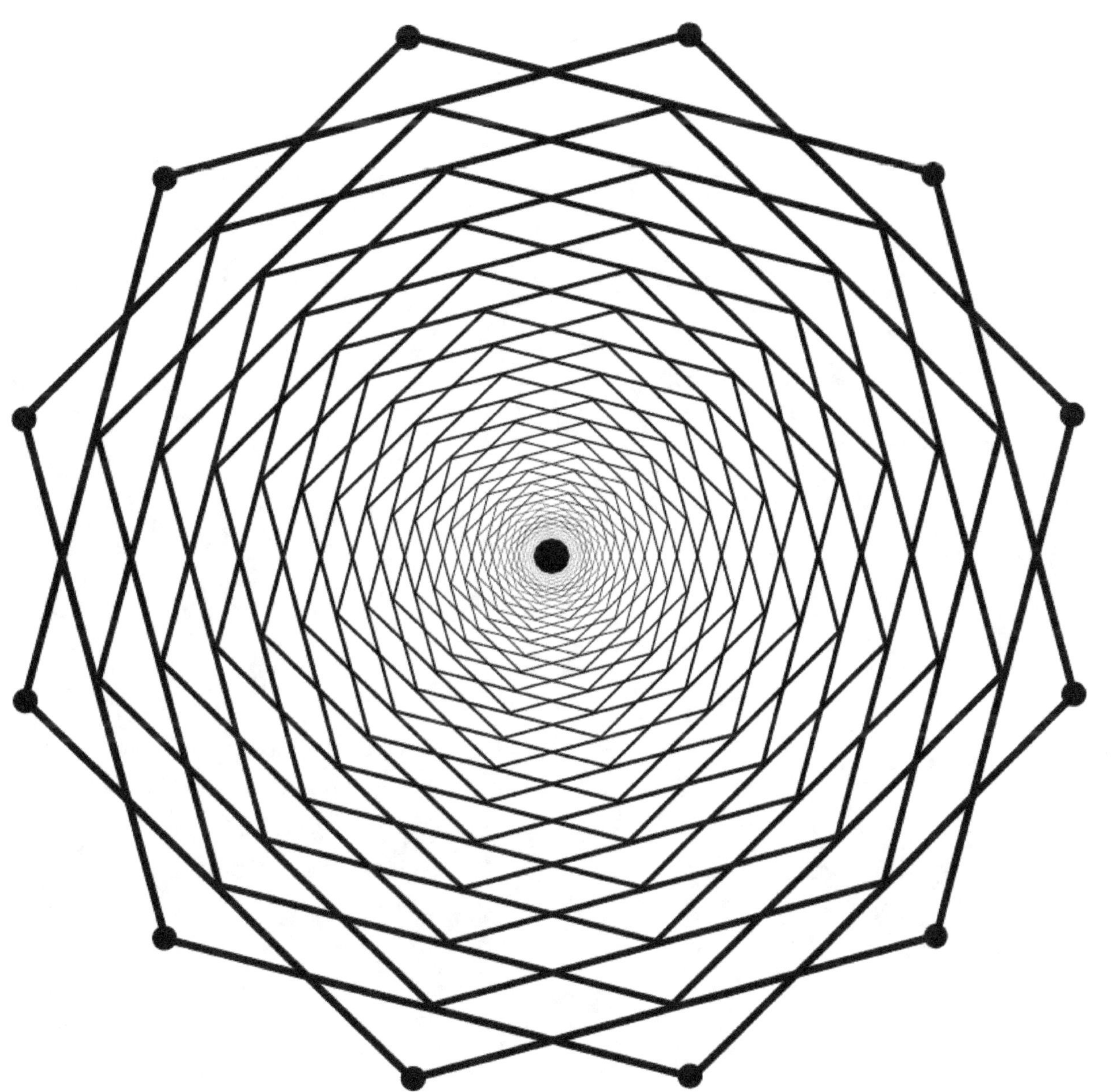

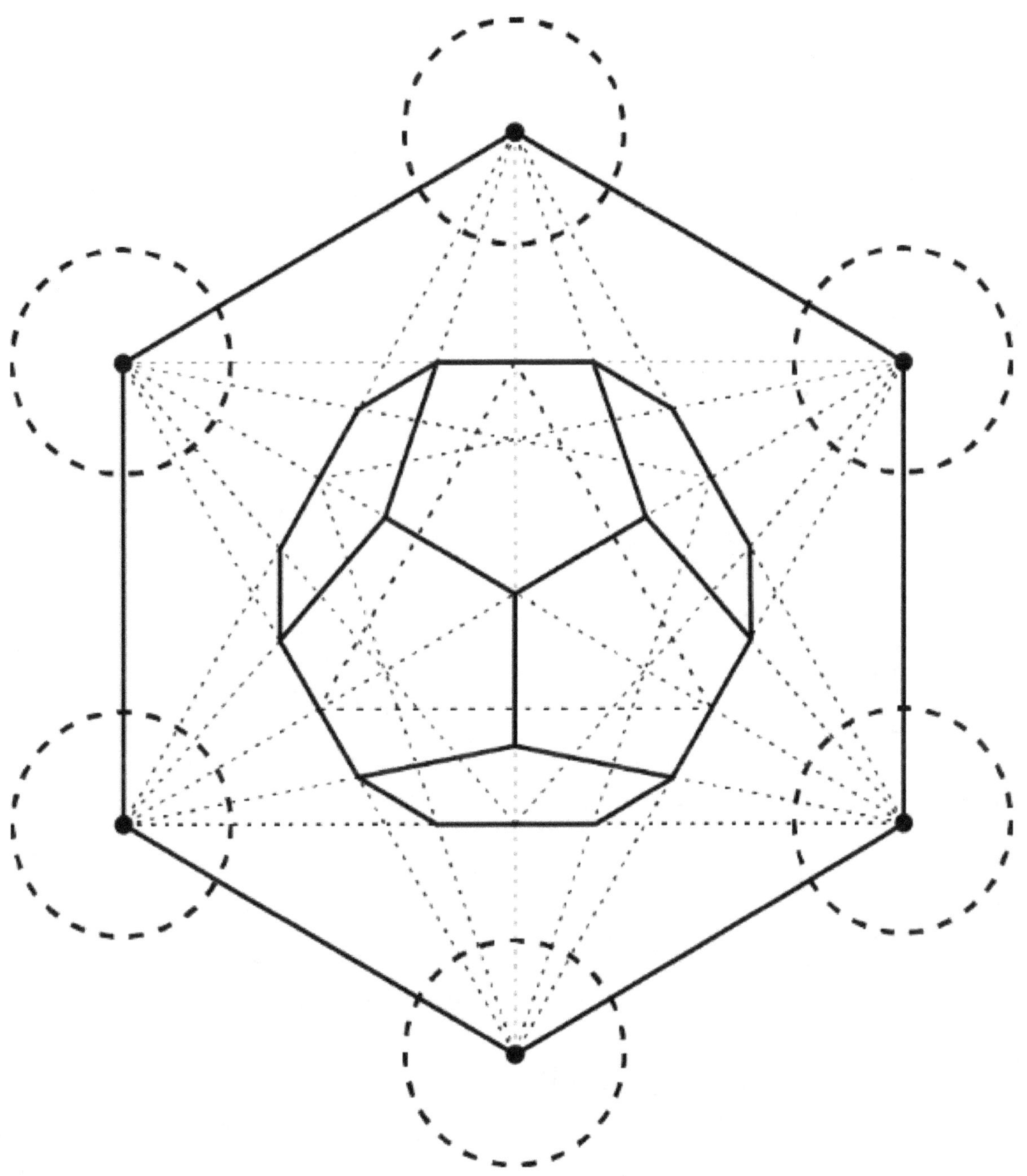

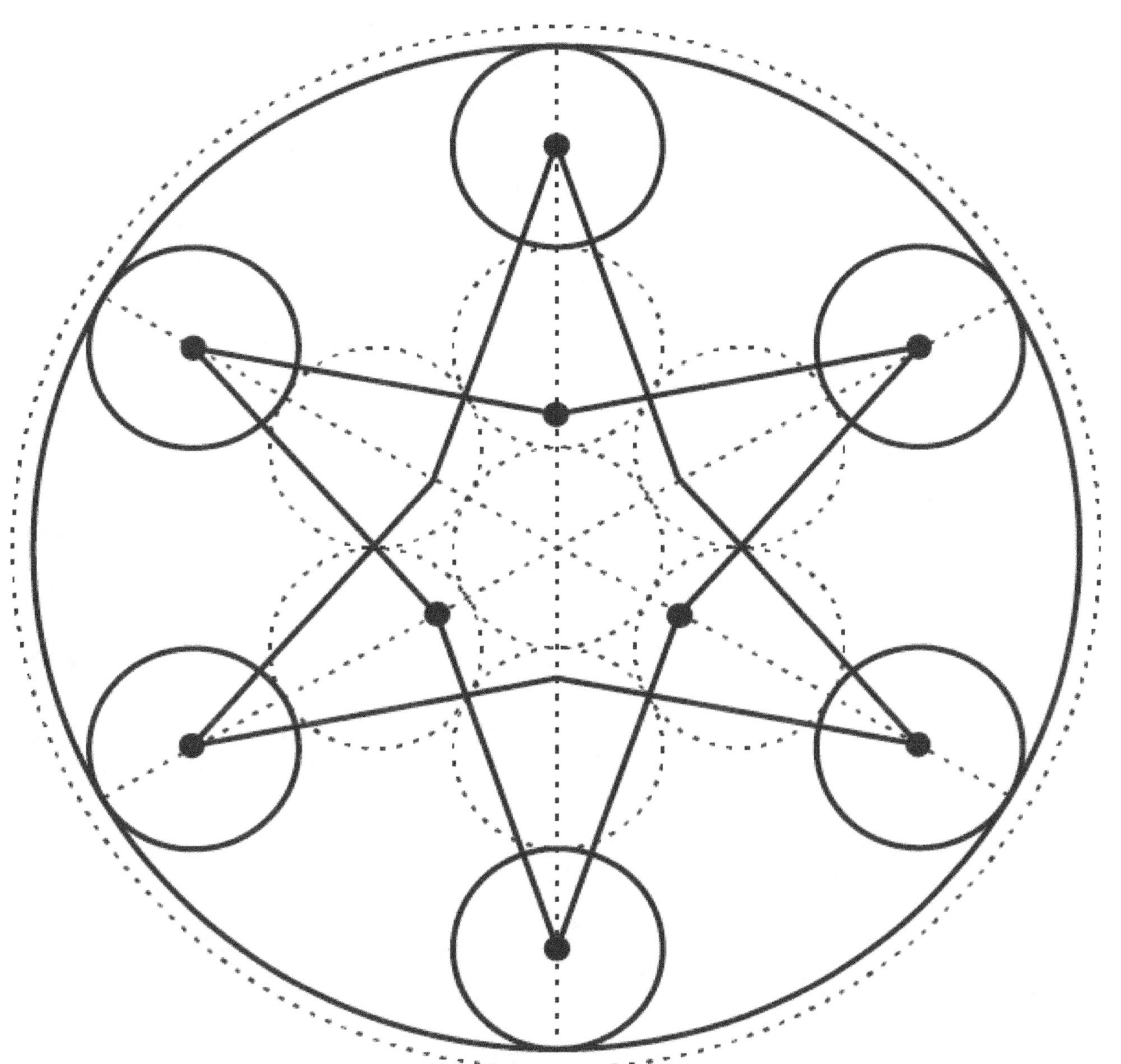

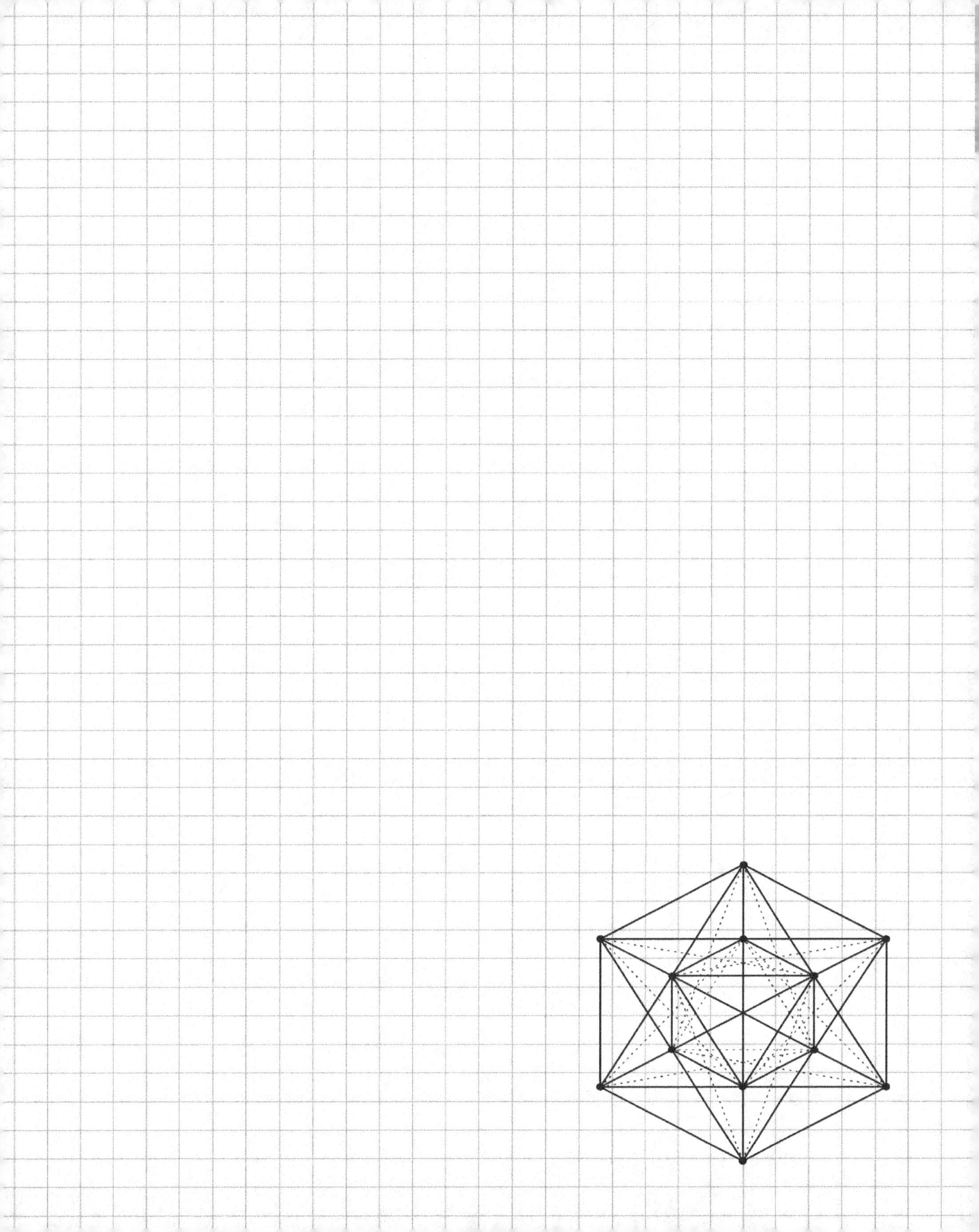

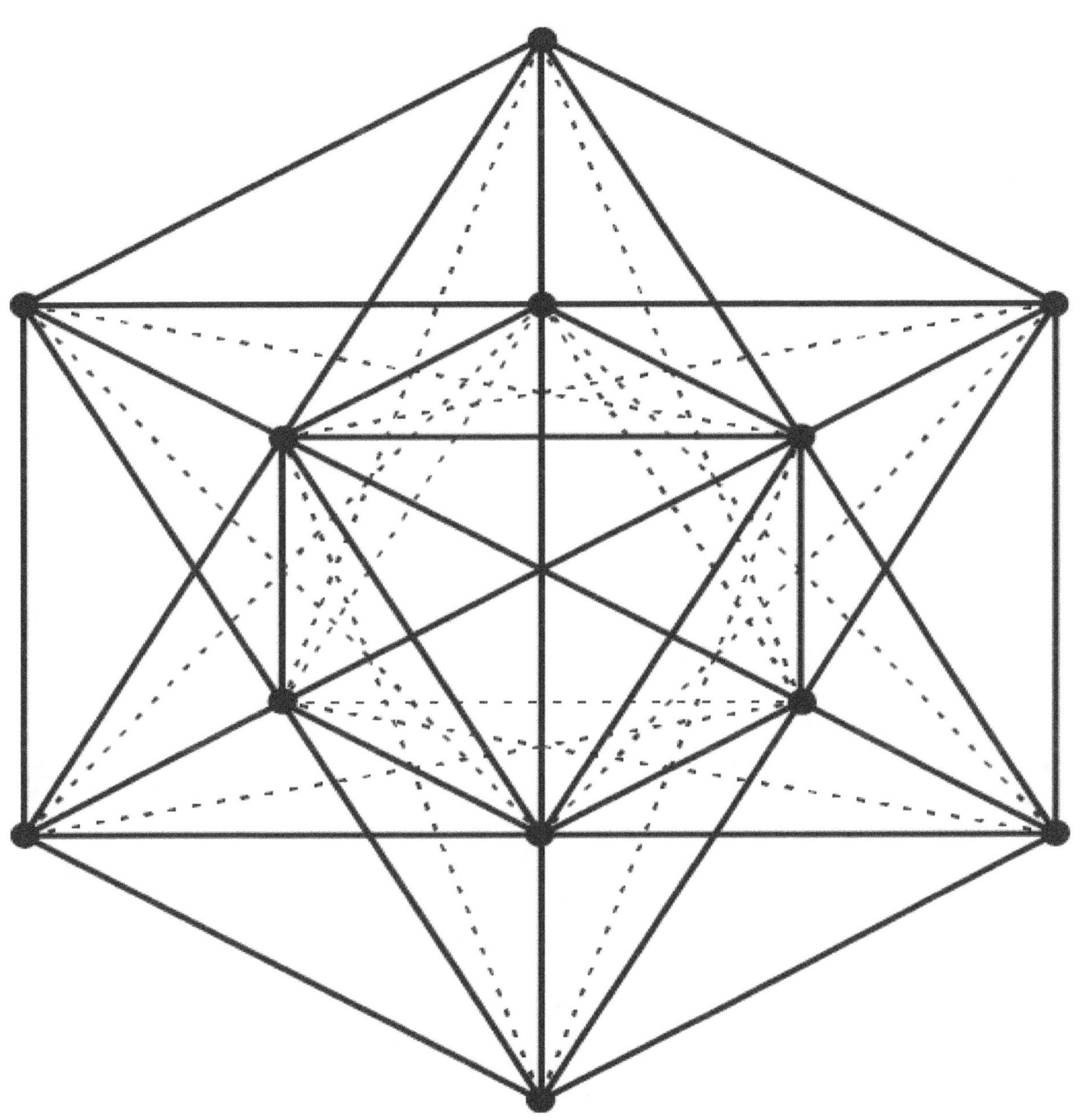

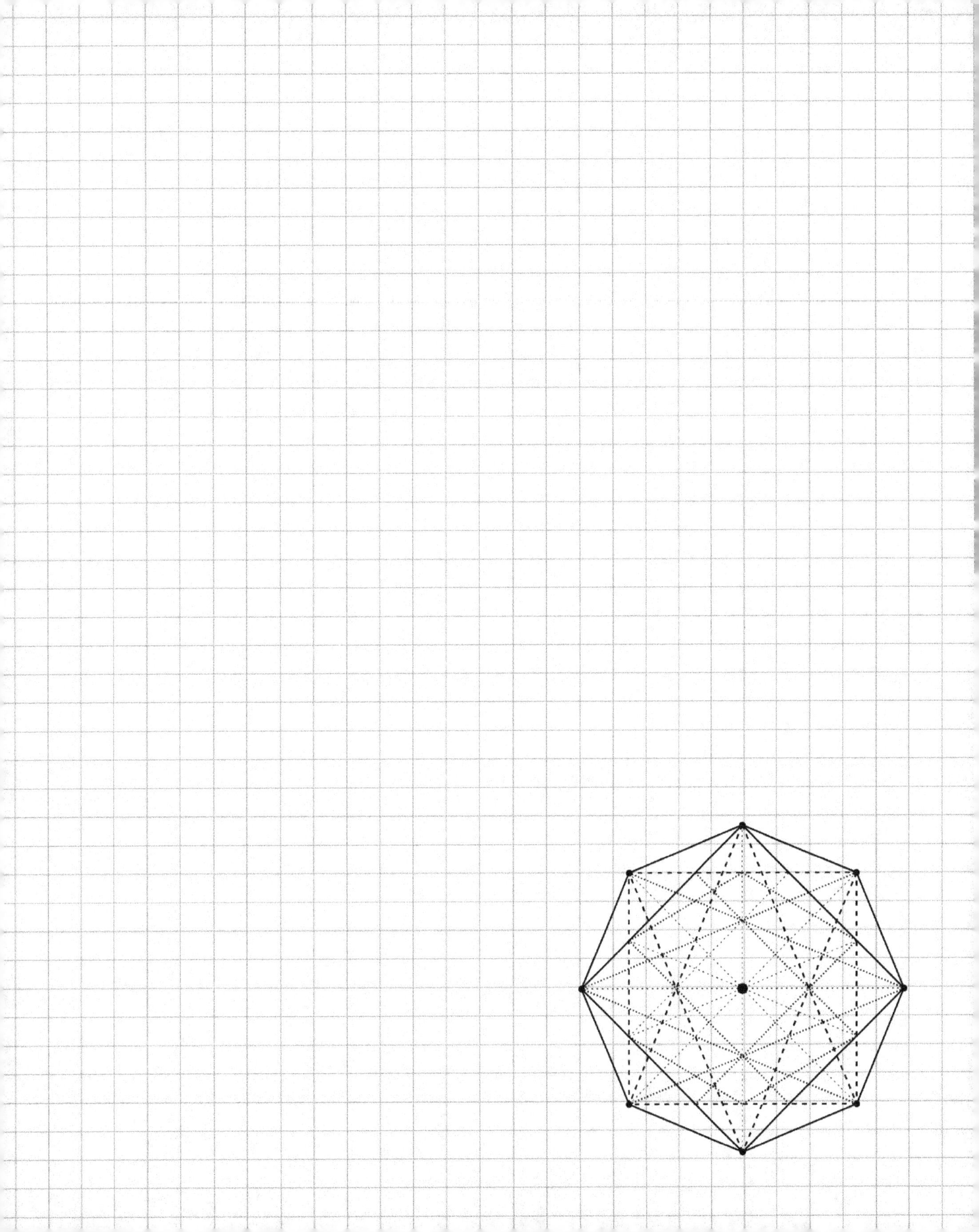

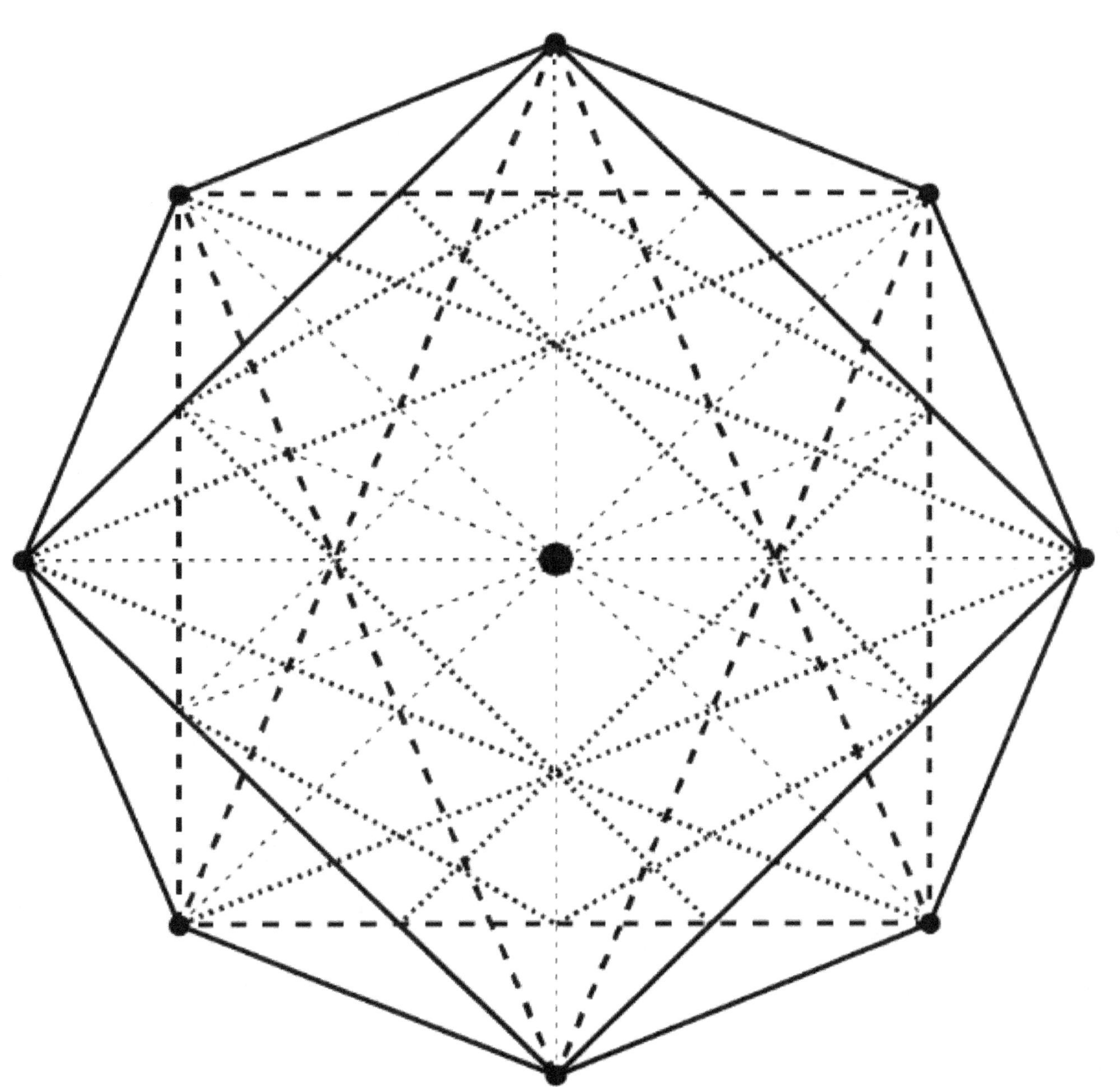

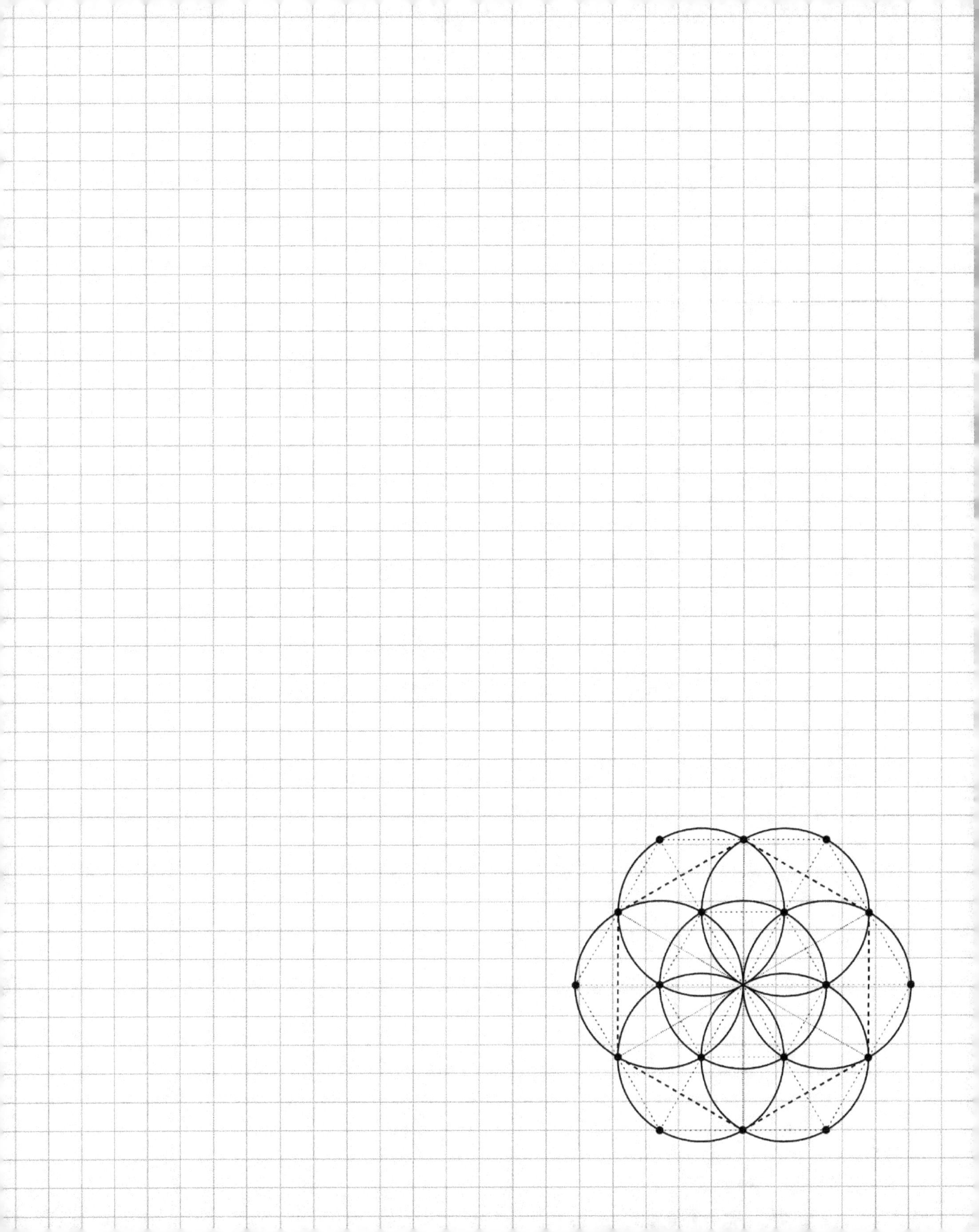

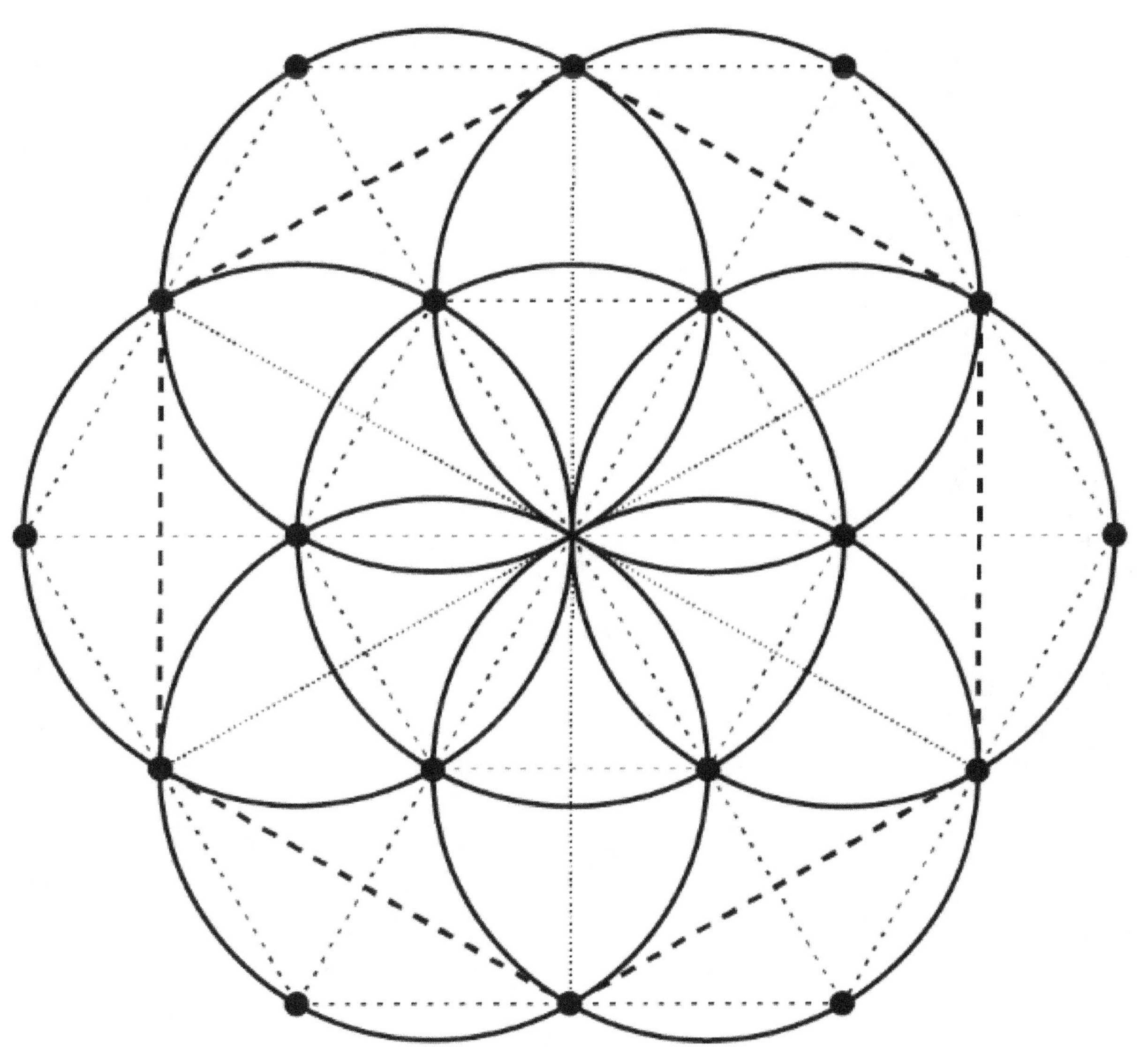

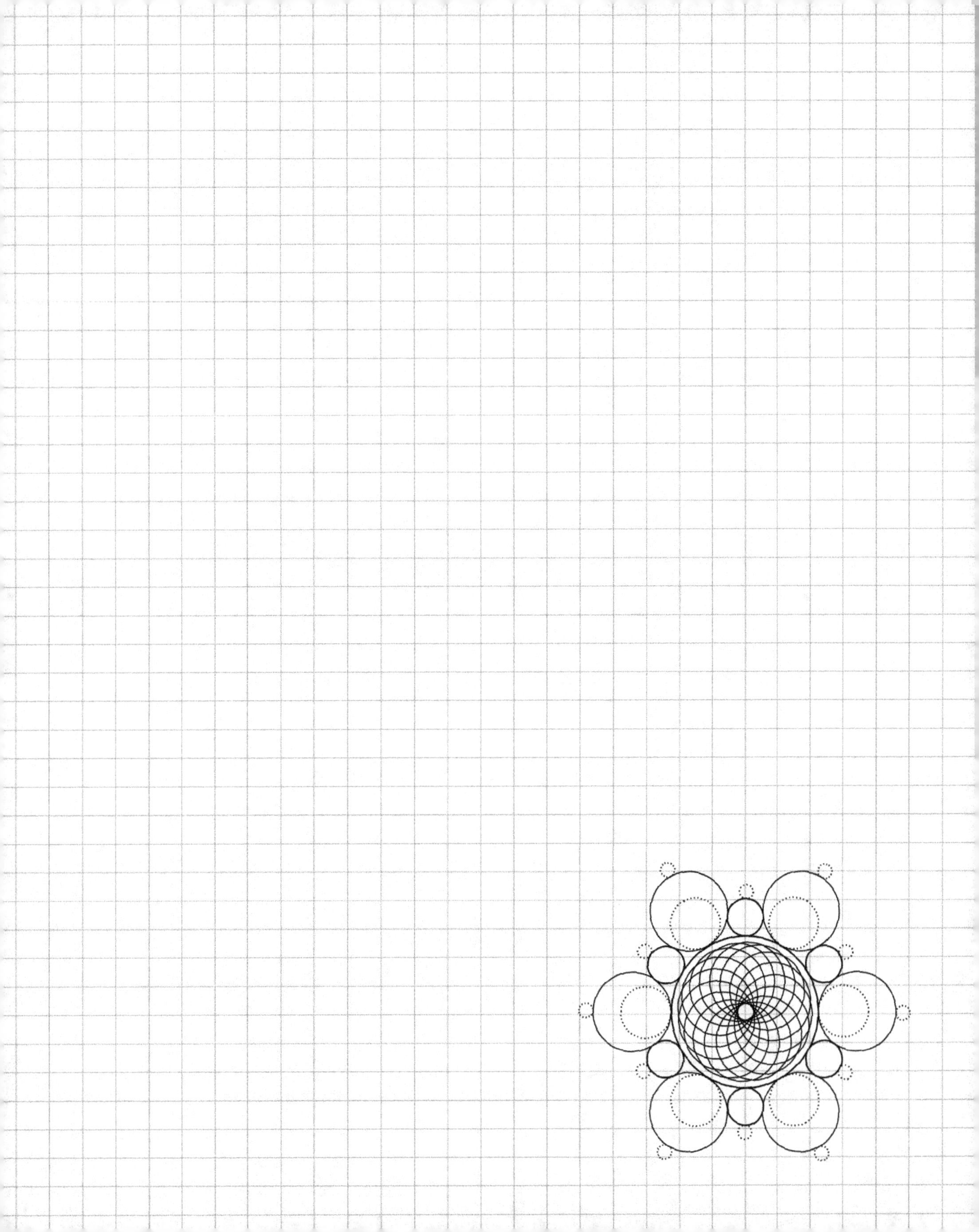

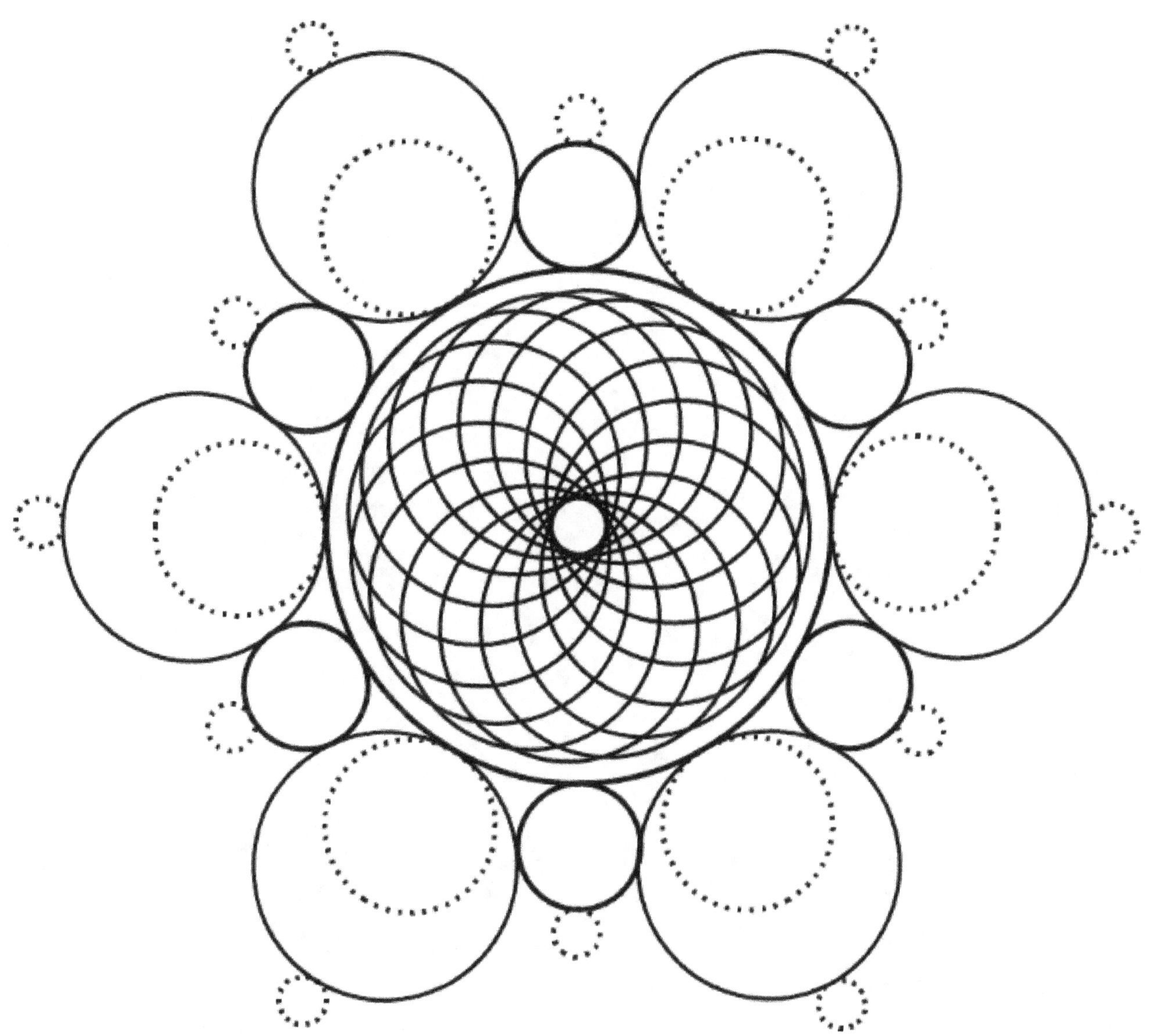

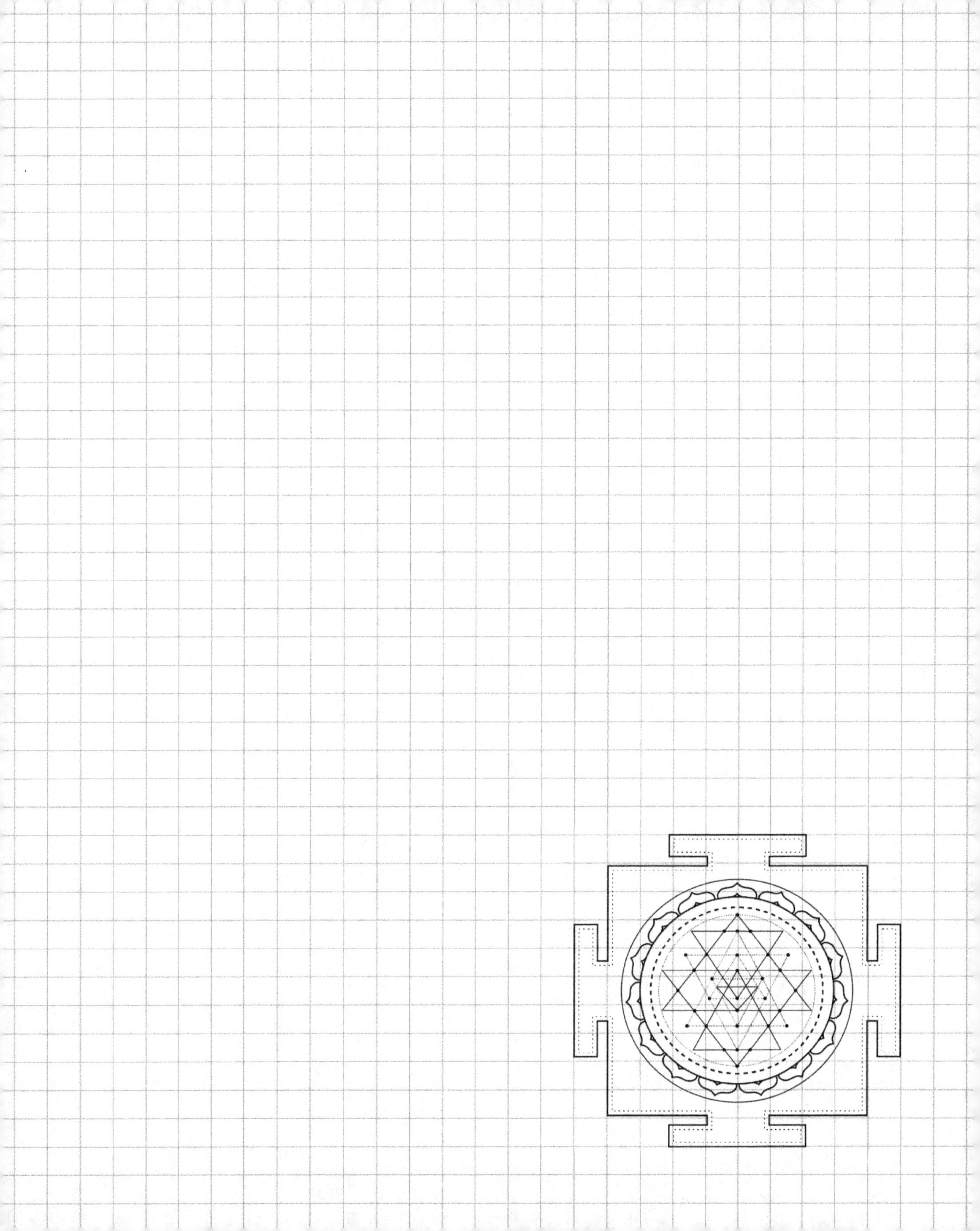

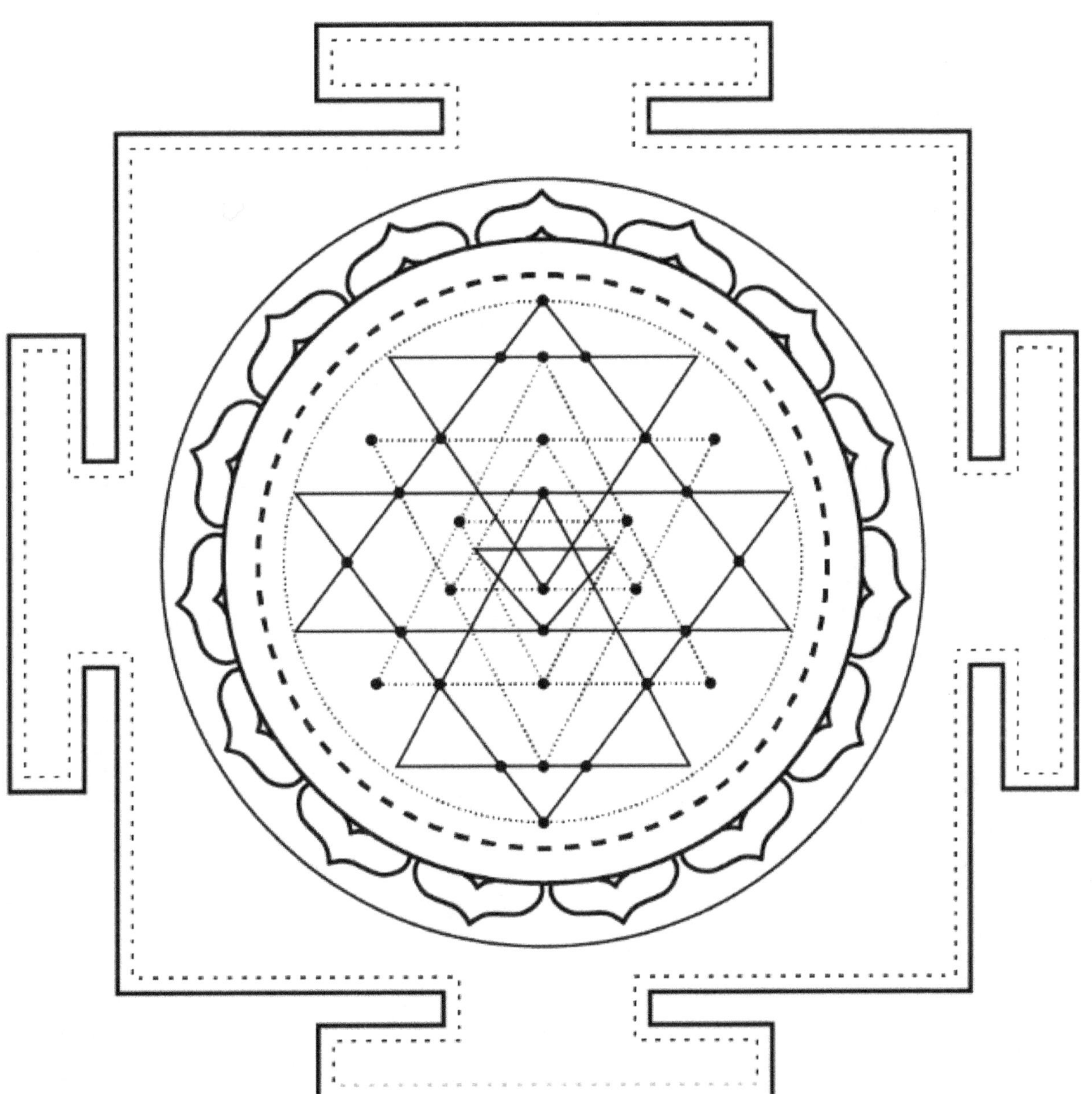

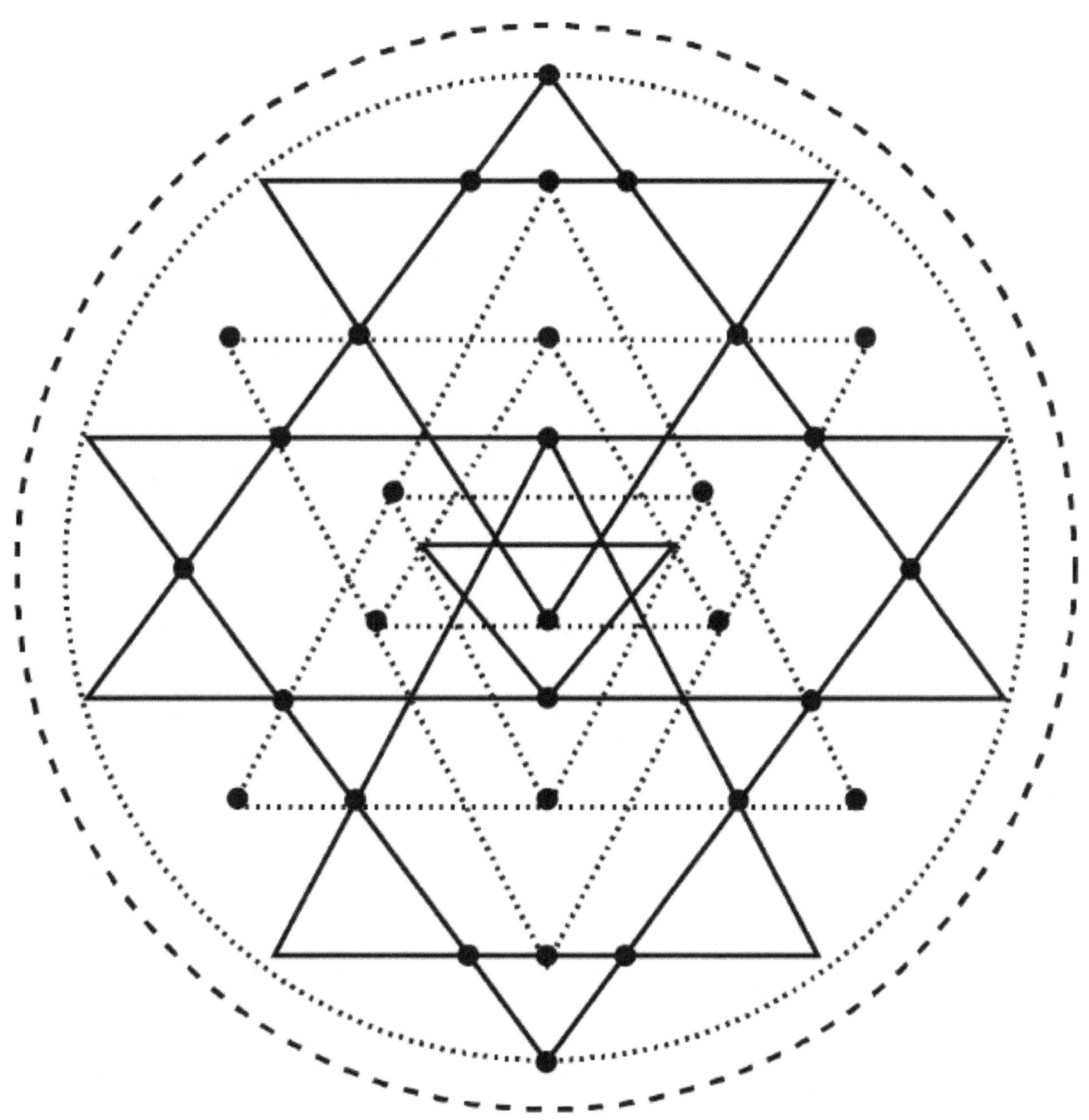

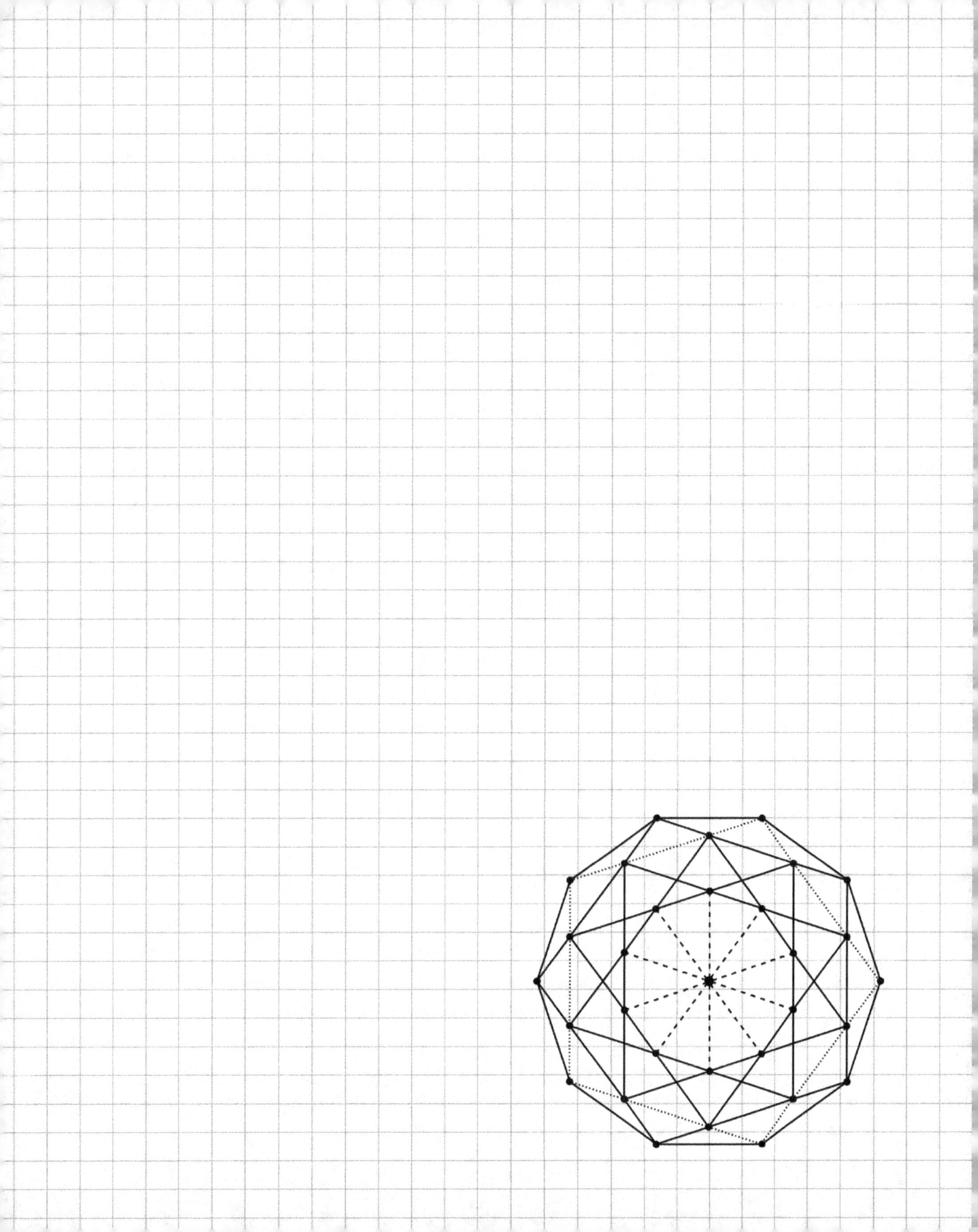

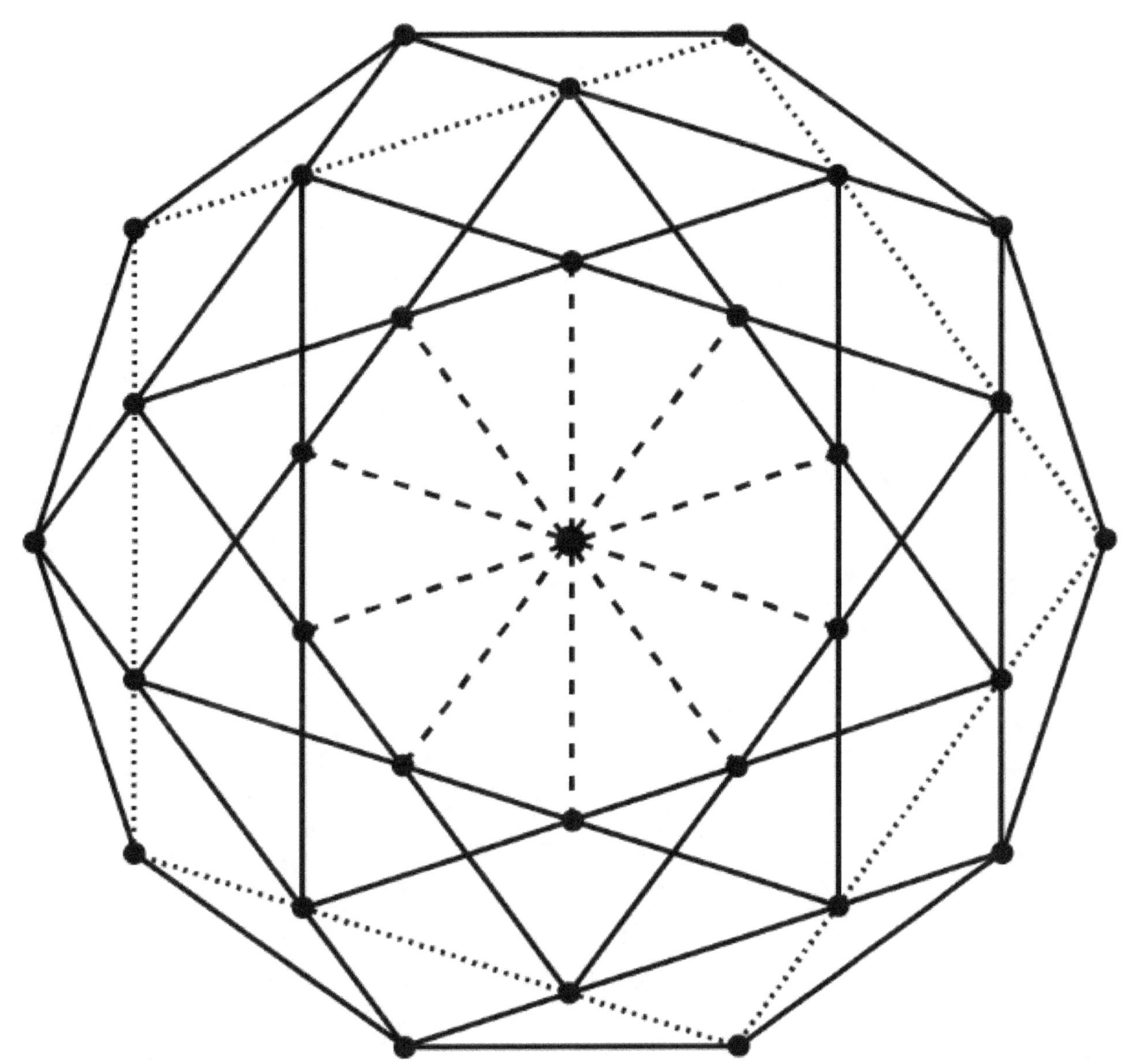

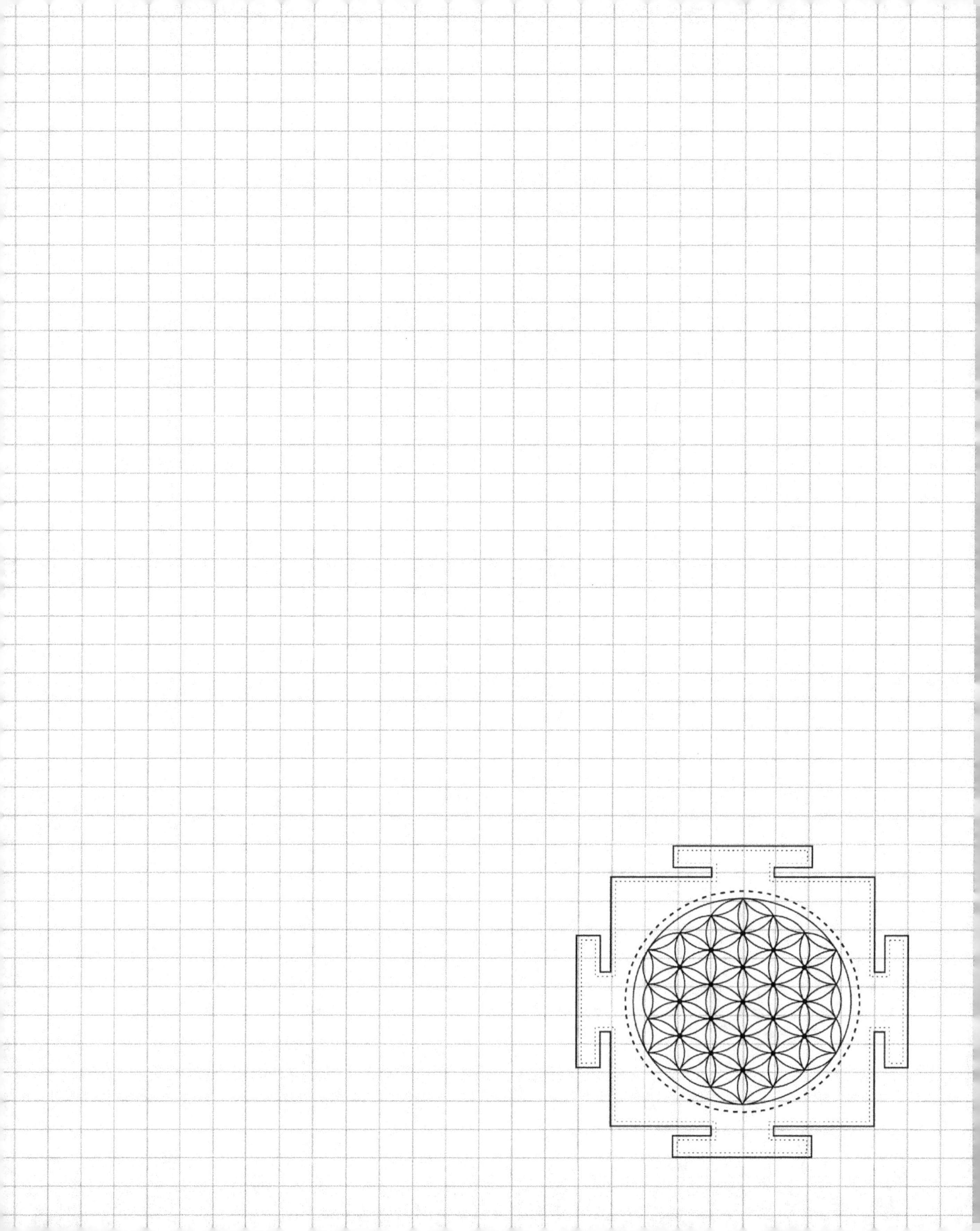

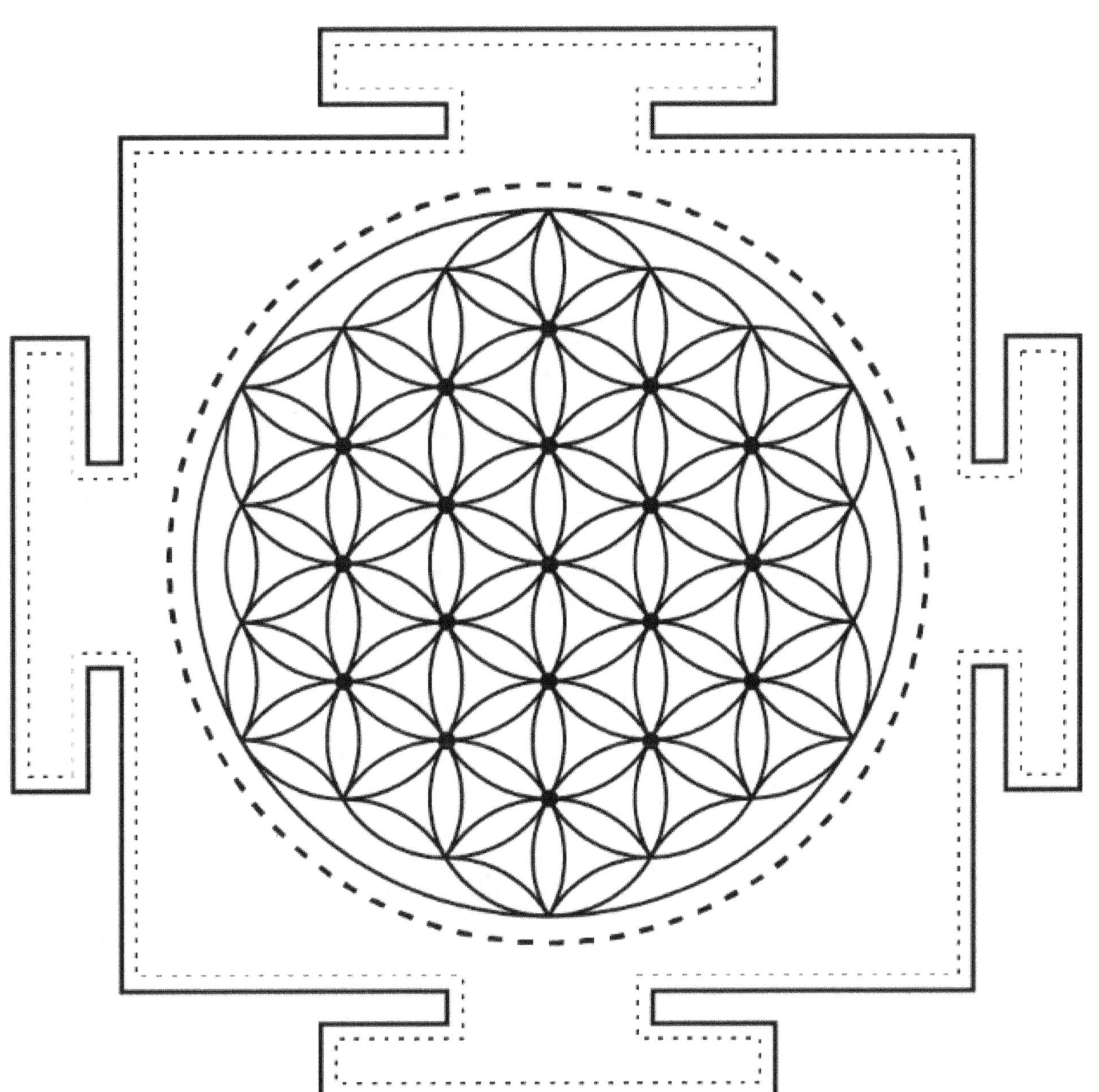

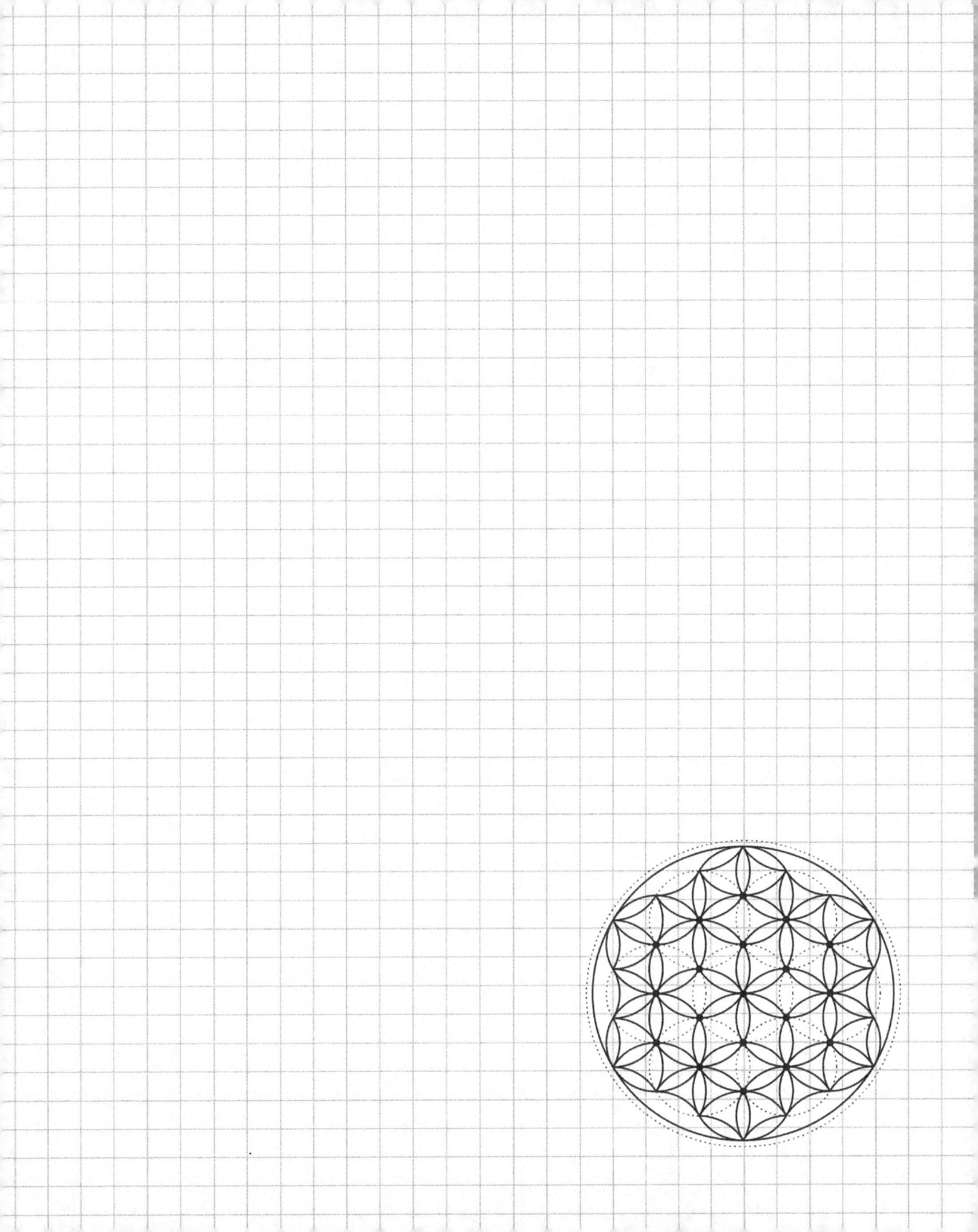

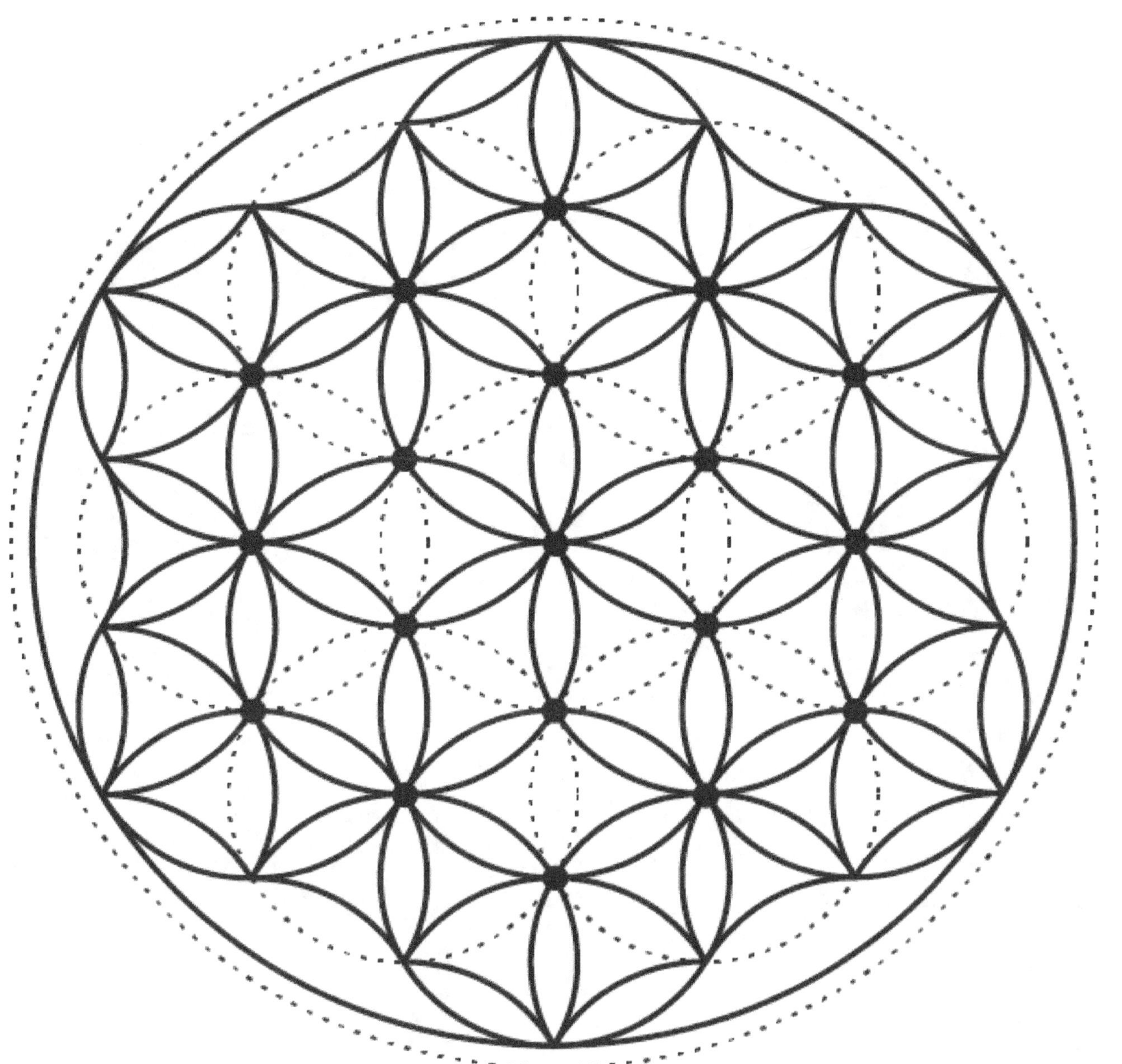

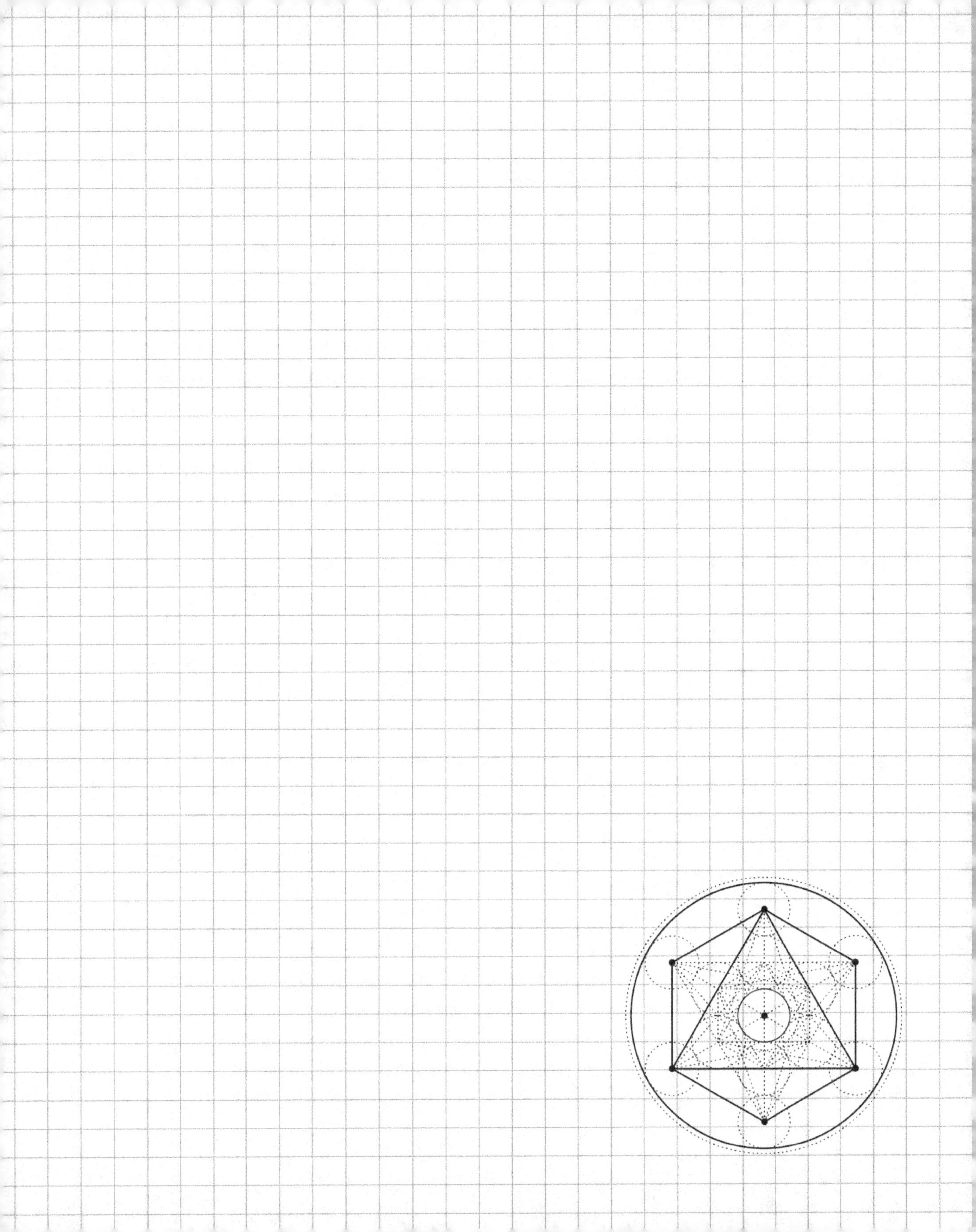

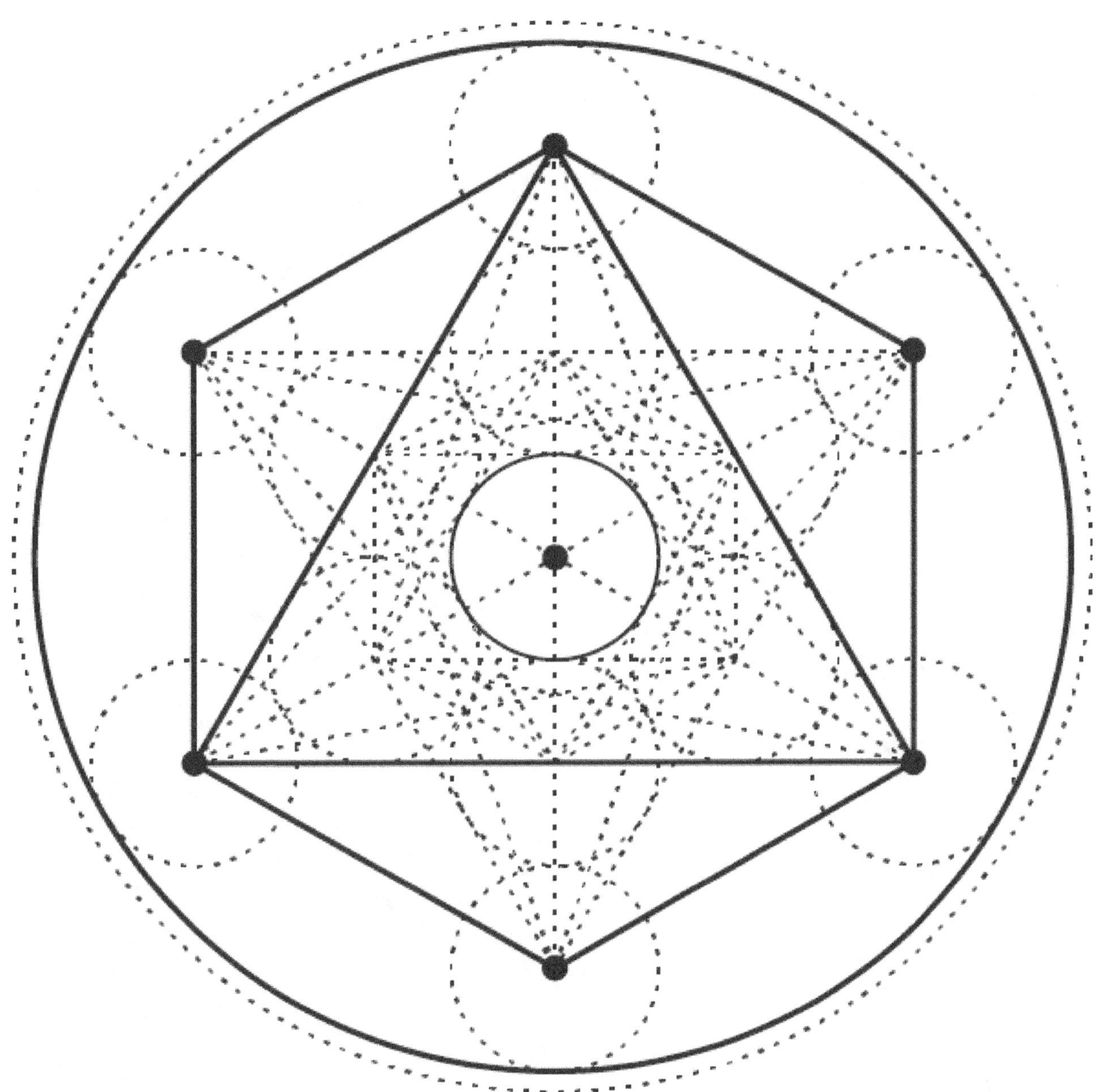